U.S. Department
of Transportation

Federal Railroad
Administration

Using Cognitive Task Analysis to Inform Issues in Human Systems Integration in Railroad Operations

Office of Research
and Development
Washington, DC 20590

U.S. Department of Transportation
Research and Special Programs Administration
John A. Volpe National Transportation Systems Center
Cambridge, MA 02142-1093

I0438601

Human Factors in Railroad Operations

DOT/FRA/ORD-13/31

Final Report
May 2013

This document is available to the
public through the National Technical Information
Service, Springfield, VA 22161.
This document is also available on the FRA Web
site at www.fra.dot.gov.

		Form Approved
REPORT DOCUMENTATION PAGE		OMB No. 0704-0188

Public reporting burden for this collection of information is estimated to average 1 hour per response, including the time for reviewing instructions, searching existing data sources, gathering and maintaining the data needed and completing and reviewing the collection of information. Send comments regarding this burden estimate or any aspects of this collection of information , including suggestions for reducing this burden to Washington Headquarters Service, Directorate for information Operations and Reports. 1215 Jefferson Davis Highway, Suite 1204, Arlington, VA. 222202-4302 and to the Office of Management and Budget. Paperwork Reduction Project (0704-0188) Washington DC 20503.

1. AGENCY USE ONLY (*LEAVE BLANK*)	2. REPORT DATE May 2013	3. REPORT TYPE AND DATES COVERED

4. TITLE AND SUBTITLE Using Cognitive Task Analysis to Inform Issues in Human Systems Integration in Railroad Operations	5. FUNDING NUMBERS RR04A3/LT278
6. AUTHOR(S) Emilie Roth, Hadar Rosenhand, and Jordan Multer	

7. PERFORMING ORGANIZATION NAME(S) AND ADDRESS(ES) U.S. Department of Transportation Research and Special Programs Administration John A. Volpe National Transportation Systems Center Cambridge, MA 02142-1093	8. PERFORMING ORGANIZATION DOT-VNTSC-FRA

9. SPONSORING/MONITORING AGENCY NAME(S) AND ADDRESS(ES) U.S. Department of Transportation Federal Railroad Administration Office of Research and Development Washington, DC 20590	10. SPONSORING/MONITORING AGENCY REPORT NUMBER DOT/FRA/ORD-13/31

11. SUPPLEMENTARY NOTES

12a. DISTRIBUTION/AVAILABILITY STATEMENT This document is available to the public through the National Technical Information Service, Springfield, VA 22161.	12b. DISTRIBUTION CODE

13. ABSTRACT (Maximum 200 words)

U. S. Railroad operations are undergoing rapid changes involving the introduction of new technologies such as positive train control (PTC), energy management systems (EMS), and electronically controlled pneumatic (ECP) brakes in the locomotive cab. To help ensure these and other new technologies are optimally designed for safe and efficient use, the Federal Railroad Administration (FRA) is interested in introducing Human Systems Integration (HSI) to the railroad industry. HSI is a systematic, organization-wide approach to implementing new technologies and modernizing existing systems that can increase the likelihood of successful deployment as well as user acceptance. This report provides guidance to the industry pertaining to the need for HSI in the technology acquisition process, and more specifically, how to use Cognitive Task Analysis (CTA) methods and results as part of the HSI process. It draws on examples from prior FRA-sponsored CTAs for locomotive engineers, conductors, dispatchers, and roadway workers to illustrate the kinds of insights that can be drawn from performing a CTA when introducing new technologies into railroad operations. The report also provides a starting point for the industry with respect to identifying likely emerging issues that need to be explored as part of the technology introduction process.

14. SUBJECT TERMS Human Factors, Cognitive Task Analysis, Human Systems Integration, HSI, Task Analysis, Locomotive Engineer, Conductor, Dispatcher, Roadway Worker, Displays, PTC, Energy Management Systems, ECP Brakes	15. NUMBER OF PAGES 56
	16. PRICE CODE

17. SECURITY CLASSIFICATION OF REPORT Unclassified	18. SECURITY CLASSIFICATION OF THIS PAGE Unclassified	19. SECURITY CLASSIFICATION OF ABSTRACT Unclassified	LIMITATION OF ABSTRACT Unclassified

NSN 7540-01-280-5500

Standard Form 298 (Rev. 2-89)
Prescribed by ANSI Std. 239-18
298-102

METRIC/ENGLISH CONVERSION FACTORS

ENGLISH TO METRIC

LENGTH (APPROXIMATE)

1 inch (in) = 2.5 centimeters (cm)

1 foot (ft) = 30 centimeters (cm)

1 yard (yd) = 0.9 meter (m)

1 mile (mi) = 1.6 kilometers (km)

AREA (APPROXIMATE)

1 square inch (sq in, in^2) = 6.5 square centimeters (cm^2)

1 square foot (sq ft, ft^2) = 0.09 square meter (m^2)

1 square yard (sq yd, yd^2) = 0.8 square meter (m^2)

1 square mile (sq mi, mi^2) = 2.6 square kilometers (km^2)

1 acre = 0.4 hectare (he) = 4,000 square meters (m^2)

MASS - WEIGHT (APPROXIMATE)

1 ounce (oz) = 28 grams (gm)

1 pound (lb) = 0.45 kilogram (kg)

1 short ton = 2,000 pounds (lb) = 0.9 tonne (t)

VOLUME (APPROXIMATE)

1 teaspoon (tsp) = 5 milliliters (ml)

1 tablespoon (tbsp) = 15 milliliters (ml)

1 fluid ounce (fl oz) = 30 milliliters (ml)

1 cup (c) = 0.24 liter (l)

1 pint (pt) = 0.47 liter (l)

1 quart (qt) = 0.96 liter (l)

1 gallon (gal) = 3.8 liters (l)

1 cubic foot (cu ft, ft^3) = 0.03 cubic meter (m^3)

1 cubic yard (cu yd, yd^3) = 0.76 cubic meter (m^3)

TEMPERATURE (EXACT)

[(x-32)(5/9)] °F = y °C

METRIC TO ENGLISH

LENGTH (APPROXIMATE)

1 millimeter (mm) = 0.04 inch (in)

1 centimeter (cm) = 0.4 inch (in)

1 meter (m) = 3.3 feet (ft)

1 meter (m) = 1.1 yards (yd)

1 kilometer (km) = 0.6 mile (mi)

AREA (APPROXIMATE)

1 square centimeter (cm^2) = 0.16 square inch (sq in, in^2)

1 square meter (m^2) = 1.2 square yards (sq yd, yd^2)

1 square kilometer (km^2) = 0.4 square mile (sq mi, mi^2)

10,000 square meters (m^2) = 1 hectare (ha) = 2.5 acres

MASS - WEIGHT (APPROXIMATE)

1 gram (gm) = 0.036 ounce (oz)

1 kilogram (kg) = 2.2 pounds (lb)

1 tonne (t) = 1,000 kilograms (kg)

= 1.1 short tons

VOLUME (APPROXIMATE)

1 milliliter (ml) = 0.03 fluid ounce (fl oz)

1 liter (l) = 2.1 pints (pt)

1 liter (l) = 1.06 quarts (qt)

1 liter (l) = 0.26 gallon (gal)

1 cubic meter (m^3) = 36 cubic feet (cu ft, ft^3)

1 cubic meter (m^3) = 1.3 cubic yards (cu yd, yd^3)

TEMPERATURE (EXACT)

[(9/5) y + 32] °C = x °F

QUICK INCH - CENTIMETER LENGTH CONVERSION

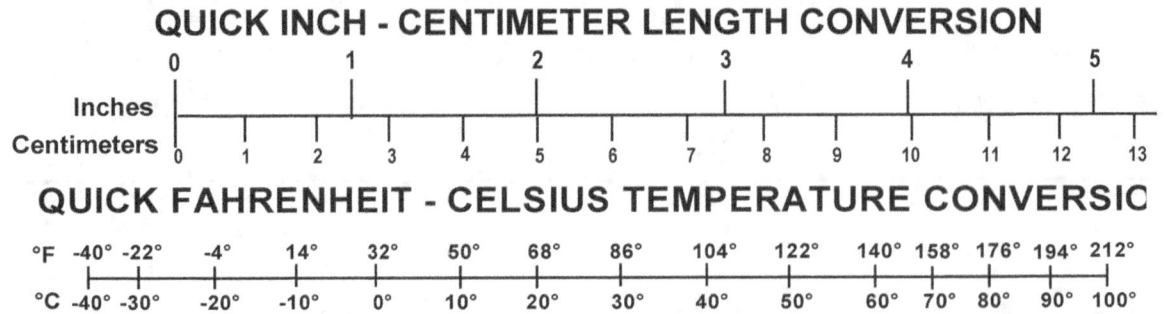

QUICK FAHRENHEIT - CELSIUS TEMPERATURE CONVERSIC

°F	-40°	-22°	-4°	14°	32°	50°	68°	86°	104°	122°	140°	158°	176°	194°	212°
°C	-40°	-30°	-20°	-10°	0°	10°	20°	30°	40°	50°	60°	70°	80°	90°	100°

For more exact and or other conversion factors, see NIST Miscellaneous Publication 286, Units of Weights and Measures. Price $2.50
SD Catalog No. C13 10286

Updated 6/17/98

ACKNOWLEDGMENTS

The Federal Railroad Administration's (FRA) Office of Research and Development funded this research effort. We wish to thank the Human Factors R&D Program, and Dr. Thomas Raslear, in particular, for the opportunity to perform cognitive analyses and inform the railroad industry of the need and methods for cognitive task analyses, specifically as it informs Human Systems Integration (HSI). Additionally, we want to thank Mr. Mike Jones of FRA's Human Factors R&D for sharing his knowledge of, and vision for, HSI in the railroad industry. Special thanks are due to Mike Coplen who early on realized the importance of cognitive task analyses and initiated this program of research at FRA.

We also want to express our thanks, again, to the railroad workers who participated in interviews and focus groups for prior cognitive task analyses. Without them, none of this would have been possible.

CONTENTS

ILLUSTRATIONS

TABLES

EXECUTIVE SUMMARY

Railroad operations in the United States are undergoing rapid changes. Perhaps the most widely anticipated change is the introduction of interfaces to new technologies such as positive train control (PTC), energy management systems (EMS), and electronically controlled pneumatic (ECP) brakes in the locomotive cab. To help ensure these and other new technologies are optimally designed for safe and efficient use, the Federal Railroad Administration (FRA) is interested in introducing Human Systems Integration (HSI) to the railroad industry. In a 2007 white paper, Reinach and Jones define HSI as a "systematic, organization-wide approach to implementing new technologies and modernizing existing systems." They note that "an HSI approach to railroad technology acquisition and implementation" can increase user acceptance and usability of the technology, as well as increase the likelihood that it is deployed successfully. This report follows the 2007 Reinach and Jones white paper and is intended to provide guidance to the industry with respect to the need for HSI in the technology acquisition process, and more specifically, how to use Cognitive Task Analysis (CTA) methods and results as part of the HSI process.

The nature of the work associated with many railway worker positions (e.g., locomotive engineers, conductors, roadway workers) is rapidly shifting from being primarily physical to placing greater emphasis on cognitive demands (e.g., monitoring, supervising automated systems, planning, communicating and coordinating, and handling unanticipated situations). CTA methods provide a means to explicitly identify the knowledge and mental processing demands of work so as to be able to anticipate contributors to performance problems (e.g., lack of information, high attention demands, inaccurate understanding) and specify ways to improve individual and team performance (be it through new forms of training, user interfaces, or decision-aids). CTAs can inform all aspects of HSI starting from early system requirements exploration and definition through late stage validation and field testing.

This report draws on examples from CTAs previously conducted by FRA for locomotive engineers, conductors, dispatchers, and roadway workers to illustrate the various ways a CTA can be used to inform the HSI process. The information contained herein is intended to serve as a lead-in to the kinds of insights that can be drawn from performing a CTA when introducing new technologies into railroad operations, as well as a starting point for the industry as far as identifying the likely emerging issues that need to be explored as a result of the introduction of new technology.

Section 2 of the report provides an introduction to HSI. Section 3 gives a brief overview of CTA methods and how they can be used to inform HSI. Section 3.2 uses examples drawn from prior railroad worker CTAs conducted by FRA to illustrate the various ways that CTAs can be used as part of the HSI process. Tables 5–8 provide concise summaries of the findings, including concrete railroad examples. Finally, using PTC and EMS as examples, Section 4 of the report discusses the issues that must be explored prior to implementing new technology.

The report concludes by laying out the various ways that CTA can inform HSI in supporting technology development and acquisition. CTA can:

1

- Define the broader context of use within which a new technology will be deployed.
- Explore implications of introduction of new technology.
- Support human factors engineering analyses.
- Inform issues of concern.

More specifically, CTAs inform HSI by:
- identifying cognitive and collaborative activities that can benefit from more effective support;
- identifying the kinds of aiding that would be most effective (e.g., the types of information that is needed and how it can best be presented);
- identifying design pitfalls to be avoided (e.g., potential negative side effects, or new cognitive and collaborative demands associated with the new technology that need to be addressed);
- mitigating the risks of design failures by promoting a more complete understanding of needs and design challenges;
- guiding mid-course design corrections and laying the groundwork for next-generation system development.

1. INTRODUCTION

Railroad operations in the United States are undergoing rapid changes. Perhaps the most widely anticipated change is the introduction of interfaces to PTC, EMS, ECP brakes, and other new technologies in the locomotive cab. To help ensure these and other new technologies are optimally designed for safe and efficient use, FRA is interested in introducing HSI to the railroad industry.

Reinach and Jones (2007) describe HSI as being a "systematic, organization-wide approach to implementing new technologies and modernizing existing systems." They further state that "it is a combination of managerial philosophy, methods, techniques, and tools designed to emphasize, during the acquisition process, the central role and importance of end-users in organizational processes or technologies." (More information about HSI can be found in Section 2.) This report is intended to inform the industry about the need for HSI in the technology acquisition process, and more specifically, to provide guidance on how to use CTA methods and results as part of the HSI process. CTA methods provide a means to explicitly identify the knowledge and mental processing demands associated with railroad worker jobs so as to be able to anticipate contributors to performance problems (e.g., lack of information, high attention demands, and inaccurate understanding) and specify ways to improve individual and team performance (be it through new forms of training, user interfaces, or decision aids). Using concrete examples drawn from the railroad industry, the report documents how CTAs can inform all aspects of HSI starting from early system requirements exploration and definition through late stage validation and field testing. (More information about CTA methods can be found in Section 3). The report also serves as a starting point for industry with respect to identifying the issues that will likely need to be explored as a result of introducing new technology.

Introduction of new technology does not necessarily guarantee improved human-machine system performance (e.g., Woods and Dekker, 2000; National Research Council, 2007; Wreathall, Woods, Bing, Christoffersen, 2007). Poor use of technology can create additional workload for system users, can result in systems that are difficult to learn or use, or, in the extreme, can result in systems that are more likely to lead to catastrophic errors (e.g., confusions that lead to pilot error and fatal aircraft accidents). Studies relating to the effect of technological change across various industries have repeatedly shown that the introduction of new technology impacts operating practice (e.g., Cook and Woods, 1996a, 1996b; Dekker and Woods, 1999; Obradovich and Woods, 1996; Smith et al., 1998; Roth, Scott, et al., 2006). Wreathall, Woods, et al. (2007) point out that common changes in operating practice that result from new technology introduction include:

- Changes in practitioner roles, including emergence of new tasks;
- Changes in what is routine and what is exceptional;
- Changes to the kinds of human errors that can occur; and
- People in their various roles adapt by actively altering tools and strategies to achieve goals and avoid failure.

These and other impacts of new technology implementation can be better anticipated by adopting a systematic, human-centered approach to system design and implementation. HSI is a discipline that seeks to anticipate and accommodate changes in practice that inevitably arise when new technology is introduced. The goal is to employ a comprehensive analysis, design, and evaluation process that mitigates the risk of designing systems that fail to meet user needs. Recently, FRA began the process of introducing HSI to the railroad industry as a way to help improve the safety and efficiency of their operations, particularly with regard to acquisition of new technology. Although the railroad industry has incorporated individual elements of HSI (for example, using human performance data collection methods to design in-cab displays), it does not currently use HSI in its technology acquisition processes (Reinach and Jones, 2007). Implementing an HSI framework would likely streamline the technology acquisition process and eliminate potential mismatches between the technology and human operator limitations or capabilities, thereby increasing safety and efficiency and reducing total costs.

As new technology is introduced, the demands associated with railroad worker positions (e.g., locomotive engineers, conductors, and roadway workers) shift from primarily physical in nature to work that is more cognitively demanding (e.g., monitoring, supervising automated systems, planning, communicating and coordinating, and handling unanticipated situations). CTA methods can play an important role in the HSI process by providing analytical tools for understanding the cognitive and collaborative demands associated with different railroad worker positions and how those demands are likely to change with the introduction of new technology. For example, CTA methods can examine how the introduction of PTC might impact the monitoring demands placed on locomotive engineers, or alter the patterns of communication between locomotive engineers and other railroad workers. CTA methods can inform the design of systems that are more likely to be successful when deployed by ensuring that they address the specific performance challenges users face and are sensitive to the larger system context.

This report contributes to the development of an HSI framework and provides guidance to the railroad industry on using CTA within the HSI process. It draws on the results of a series of railroad worker CTAs that were sponsored by FRA's Office of Research and Development as part of its efforts to investigate the safety implications of operational changes and emerging technologies. The first CTA focused on railroad dispatchers (Roth, Malsch, and Multer, 2001). A second CTA addressed roadway worker activities (Roth and Multer, 2007). The third report documented the results of a CTA that was conducted to examine the cognitive and collaborative demands and activities of locomotive engineers (Roth and Multer, 2009). The last report to date examined the cognitive and collaborative activities of freight train conductors (Rosenhand, Roth, and Multer 2012).

To help provide the industry with guidance on best practices in new technology implementation, FRA has sponsored two companion CTA synthesis reports that will examine findings from across the four previously conducted CTAs that may inform the industry on relevant emerging topics. The present report draws on examples from the four FRA-sponsored railroad worker CTAs to illustrate the various ways in which a CTA can be used to inform successful deployment of new technology as part of a comprehensive HSI process. The report is intended to serve as an introduction to the kinds of insights that can be drawn from performing a CTA when introducing new technologies into railroad operations, as well as a starting point for industry with respect to identifying the issues that will likely need to be explored as a result of the introduction of new technology. A second report will focus on issues related to teamwork, specifically communication and coordination within and across different railroad industry crafts (e.g., dispatchers, roadway workers, and train crews). It will draw on examples from previous CTAs to illustrate how new technology can impact teamwork processes (both positively and negatively). The report will also discuss the importance of considering support for teamwork processes as part of HSI and design of new technologies.

Section 2 of this report provides an introduction to HSI. Section 3 gives a brief overview of CTA methods and how they can be used to inform HSI. Section 3.2 uses examples drawn from prior railroad worker CTAs conducted by FRA to illustrate the various ways that CTAs can be used as part of the HSI process. Tables 5–8 provide concise summaries of the findings, including concrete railroad examples. Finally, Section 4 of the report discusses the issues that must be explored prior to implementing new technology, using PTC and EMS as examples. The report concludes by laying out the various ways that CTA can inform HSI in supporting technology development and acquisition.

2. HUMAN SYSTEMS INTEGRATION

HSI is a systematic organization-wide approach to implementing new technologies and modernizing existing systems that emphasizes the importance of the end-user in the system acquisition process (Reinach and Jones, 2007). HSI underscores the need to consider the broader system (i.e., the individuals and groups that are part of the system and the interaction between them and the technology) of which the technology is only one part. HSI considers the joint person-technology system the relevant unit for analysis, design, and evaluation. It encompasses both the operational and maintenance needs associated with the new technology and implications for staffing and training of personnel, as well as design of the equipment and user interfaces.

HSI is first and foremost a *life-cycle systems engineering process*. It begins during the initial capability and requirements gathering phase and continues through the design and construction phases and on through deployment and operational feedback. HSI also emphasizes *systems integration* to ensure that the individual elements of the system are not analyzed and designed in isolation one from the other, but as an integrated whole. For example, with the design of the physical equipment, the different pieces that might be installed in a locomotive cab need to be considered as a unified system, and the potential for interaction among those pieces needs to be explicitly examined. Examples of negative interactions to be alert for include excessive workload when trying to monitor and respond to the different displays in a locomotive cab and the possibility that the different displays provide contradictory or conflicting information or guidance. Accordingly, HSI advocates an integrated analysis and development approach across the different human performance-related 'domains' that are involved in HSI. For example, it advocates consolidation and collaboration when performing analyses of staffing needs, training requirements, human-interface design, maintenance needs, and safety analyses.

The first major organization to implement HSI concepts was the U.S. Army when it created the Manpower and Personnel Integration (MANPRINT) management and technical program in 1986 (Booher, 2003). MANPRINT specifies seven domains including manpower, personnel, training, and human factors engineering that need to be considered as part of a systematic HSI process (a fuller description of the MANPRINT domain-oriented approach is provided in Section 2.2.1.) Since the Army first implemented MANPRINT, HSI has become a more widely accepted concept. For example, a board on HSI has been set up as part of the Behavioral and Social Sciences and Education Division of the National Research Council, and organizations are increasingly incorporating HSI into their system acquisition process, or including it as criteria in system and program evaluation (Booher, 2003; O'Hara et al., 2004; National Research Council Committee, 2007). Although different organizations incorporate somewhat different domains or activities into their HSI process, they all share a core commitment to a systems-orientation and a user-centered approach.

In this section, we provide an introduction to HSI and present several approaches to HSI that have been successfully adopted by different military, government, and industrial organizations. The aim is to introduce the range of human factors domains of concern (e.g., manpower, personnel selection, training, human factors engineering) and human factors activities (e.g., operating experience review, function analysis and allocation, task analysis, human factors design, verification and validation) that need to be considered as part of a comprehensive HSI process. In section 3, we discuss how CTA can inform these various elements of HSI.

It should be noted that while HSI is particularly relevant to new technology acquisition, it is not limited to development of new technologies. It is intended be applied anytime a meaningful change to the system occurs; for example, adjustments to manpower or procedural changes all impact the larger system development process. The end goal of HSI is to optimize performance and minimize life-cycle ownership cost by enhancing whole system safety and efficiency (Reinach and Jones, 2007).

2.1   CORE GOALS AND ELEMENTS OF HSI

Booher (2003) presents a high-level model that emphasizes the core goals and elements of HSI (See Figure 1). The initial input is information about the system definition, development, and deployment plan. The HSI considerations are the two inputs on either side of the HSI process box. They include: 1) taking a highly concentrated user focus approach and 2) making use of human related technologies and disciplines in the design and implementation of the final product. The output of the HSI process, then, is a systems integration of people, technology, and organization. Booher (2003) argues that any design process that incorporates the elements in this high-level model will most likely take adequate consideration of the end-user.

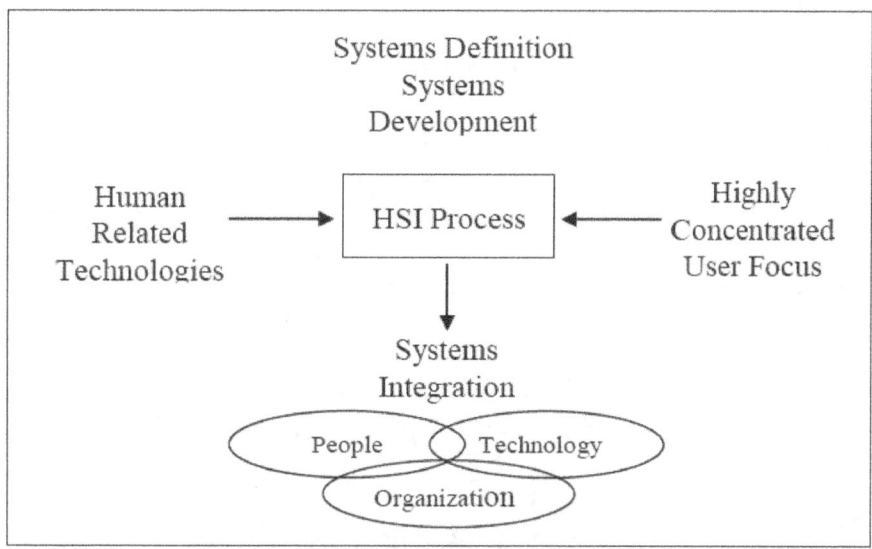

Figure 1. Human systems integration model (Booher, 2003)

A number of specific HSI frameworks have been developed for achieving the goals embodied in Booher's HSI model. For example, the Army's MANPRINT defines specific *domains of analysis* where human performance considerations apply (e.g., manpower, personnel, training, human-factors engineering) that need to be included as part of a comprehensive HSI. There have also been other perspectives that more explicitly call out the *analysis activities* that must be performed (e.g., operating experience review, function allocation, task analysis) as part of a comprehensive HSI. This perspective, used by the Nuclear Regulatory Commission (NRC), for example, provides a roadmap of specific activities that must be performed as part of HSI. While these perspectives provide alternative ways of characterizing the scope of HSI, both perspectives encompass much the same human performance considerations and require that the same types of human factors methods and analyses are performed.

The following sections provide an overview of each of these perspectives to HSI. Since there is no single, prescribed method for implementing HSI, the railroad industry can draw from these multiple perspectives in developing its own unique framework.

2.1.1 Domains of Analysis

The U.S. Army was the first institution to specify domains, or topical areas, within its HSI program that had to be considered prior to approving, acquiring, or deploying a new technology. The specified areas were Manpower, Personnel, Training, Human Factors Engineering, System Safety, Health Hazards, and Survivability. The domains are explained briefly in table 1 below.

Table 1. U.S. Army HSI (MANPRINT) Domains (Booher, 2003)

Domain	Description
Manpower	The number of human resources required and available to operate and maintain the system.
Personnel	The human characteristics necessary to achieve optimal system performance.
Training	The knowledge, skills, and abilities needed by the personnel to operate and maintain systems.
Human Factors Engineering	The comprehensive incorporation of personnel into defining, designing, developing, and evaluating the system to optimize the performance of human-machine interaction.
System Safety	The intrinsic ability of the system to operate and be maintained without accidental injury to personnel.
Health Hazards	The intrinsic conditions in the operation or use of a system that pose hazards to the personnel (e.g., death, injury, illness, disability) or reduce job performance.
Soldier Survivability	The characteristic of a system that can reduce detectability, attack, damage, injury, and physical and mental fatigue of the soldier.

The MANPRINT domains, or some variation of them, have since been adopted by several other organizations, including the U.S. Department of Defense (DoD), the UK Ministry of Defence (MOD), and the Canadian armed forces (Defence Research and Development Canada) (Reinach and Jones, 2007).

Though the number and language of the domains differ across institutions, the idea behind this perspective remains the same; the goal is to ensure that the end-user is continuously considered in developing or acquiring systems. To that end, a number of specific human factors activities are often called out to be performed (Malone, Savage-Knepshield and Avery, 2007). They include:

- Preparing an HSI plan that describes and schedules HSI domain activities and products and the points of interaction across domains;
- Collecting and tracking operations and maintenance feedback and lessons learned from prior (legacy) systems;
- Conducting a top-down requirements analysis that addresses requirements and concepts for each HSI domain;
- Maintaining a consolidated database capturing HSI assumptions, issues, questions, expected problems, risks, concepts, and criteria concerning all aspects of human involvement in the system;
- Applying modeling and simulation techniques to develop and assess derived requirements, design concepts, and criteria, including task modeling, workload assessment, and human-in the-loop simulation;
- Developing designs (including human-machine interfaces) that address requirements for human performance, competence, health and safety, and accommodation;
- Conducting person-in-the-loop test and evaluation activities focused on assessing the adequacy of the joint person-technology system for meeting overall system and human-performance requirements.

2.1.2 Analysis Activities

While MANPRINT and related HSI approaches characterize HSI in terms of the domains of concern and the need for interaction across them, other approaches have focused more on defining the human factors analyses or activities that need to be performed to uncover HSI concerns. This perspective is intended as a complement to the domains of analysis perspective.

The Committee on Human-System Design Support for Changing Technology, sponsored by the National Research Council, the operating arm of the National Academies, defines three classes of activities to be used in uncovering HSI concerns (NAS, 2007). These activities encompass human factors methods to accomplish the following:

1. *Define opportunities and context of use*—used to provide information about user characteristics, user tasks, and the broader environment in which they operate.
2. *Define requirements and design solutions*—used to identify system requirements and design alternatives.
3. *Evaluate*—used to evaluate the acceptability of the proposed design solutions and, if necessary, drive further design solutions.

Each of these activities is associated with human factors methods and analyses. For example, CTA plays a significant role in defining opportunities and context of use. As you will see in the rest of this report, it can also be used to inform design requirements and specify evaluation needs.

A key point stressed by the NAS committee is that the three classes of activities are not sequential, but proceed in parallel fashion, each with greater or less intensity depending on the system life-cycle phase (see Figure 2 below). For example, activities associated with defining opportunities and context of use are more likely to be carried out early in system development; therefore, the activity level is highest early on. However, because context of use is constantly evolving, it is important to continue to devote some effort to understanding context of use as the system continues to be developed, tested, and fielded—the effort required may decrease as the process continues. Also, as shown in the figure below, activities related to requirements definition and solution development will tend to be at the highest level of intensity toward the middle of the development cycle when design concepts are being fleshed out and prototypes are being developed and tested. However, new requirements are likely to continue to be uncovered and designs refined throughout the life cycle. Evaluation activities will tend to be highest later in the life cycle once a design is mature enough to be tested, but some evaluation activity is likely to start early (e.g., rapid prototype testing) and continue through system fielding.

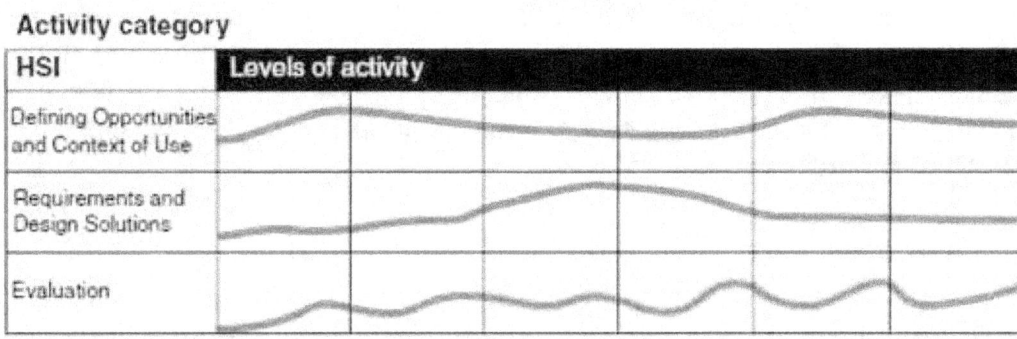

Figure 2. Activity level of HSI methods across system life-cycle phases (NAS, 2007)

As previously mentioned, the NRC is another organization that has adopted HSI as a means to promote safer, more effective systems. The NRC developed a program review model that defines a detailed list of human factors activities that need to be performed as part of the design and evaluation of a complex system. Although the program review model was developed to support regulators in conducting reviews of design certification submittals, it also provides useful guidance for system developers on the human factors activities that need to be conducted as part of a comprehensive HSI program. The 12 human factors activities in the NRC review criteria and their objectives are described in Table 2 below.

Table 2. NRC Review Criteria

	Human Factors Activity	Objective
1.	*Human Factors Engineering (HFE) Program Management*	The objective of this activity is to ensure that there is a HFE design team with the responsibility and authority to provide reasonable assurance that designs are consistent with HFE standards.
2.	*Operating Experience Review*	The objective of this activity is to ensure that HFE-related problems and issues in prior designs or systems have been identified and analyzed to avoid negative features associated with predecessor designs.
3.	*Function Analysis and Allocation*	The objective of this activity is to ensure that a functional analysis is conducted and that function allocations take advantage of human strengths and avoid allocating functions that would be negatively affected by human limitations.
4.	*Task Analysis*	The objective of this activity is to ensure a task analysis is completed to identify task requirements necessary to accomplish the functions identified in the function analysis and allocation.
5.	*Staffing and Qualifications*	The objective of this activity is to perform analyses to determine the requirements for number and qualifications of personnel.
6.	*Human Reliability Analysis*	The objective of this activity is to evaluate and address potential for human error to minimize the likelihood of personnel error and ensure that errors are detected and recovered from.
7.	*Human-System Interface (HFE) Design*	The objective of this activity is to ensure that functional and task requirements have been appropriately translated to design requirements and that the design meets human factors engineering standards.
8.	*Procedure Development*	The objective of this activity is to ensure that human engineering principles and guidance are applied to develop procedures that are technically accurate, comprehensive, explicit, easy to use, and validated.
9.	*Training Program Development*	The objective of this activity is to ensure that sufficient personnel training is developed and implemented in a manner consistent with HFE principles and practices.
10.	*Verification and Validation*	The objective of this activity is (1) to verify that the human-system interface supports personnel task requirements (as defined by the task analysis), (2) to verify that the human-system interface is designed to

		accommodate human capabilities and limitations, and (3) to perform a validation study using performance-based tests to determine whether the integrated system design meets performance requirements.
11.	*Design Implementation*	The objective of this activity is to ensure that the implemented design conforms to the verified and validated design that came out of the HFE design process. This activity also encompasses the kinds of activities associated with design deployment.
12.	*Human Performance Monitoring*	The objective of this activity is to implement a human performance monitoring strategy to ensure that safety degradation does not occur over time and that personnel have maintained the necessary skills to accomplish their tasks.

Throughout the paper we will be referring back to both domains and activities to point out where CTA methods can have value.

3. OVERVIEW OF COGNITIVE TASK ANALYSIS GOALS AND METHODS

CTA is a way to identify and take into account the cognitive requirements inherent in performing complex work (Potter et al., 2000; Schraagen et al., 2000). Bisantz and Roth (2008) provide a comprehensive overview of CTA methods and their rationale. Crandall, Klein and Hoffman (2006) provide a detailed practitioner's guide to performing a CTA.

The need to perform CTAs arises from the changing nature of the work associated with many railway worker positions. In many cases, the work for railroad workers (e.g., locomotive engineers, conductors, roadway workers) is rapidly shifting from primarily physical in nature to work that places a greater emphasis on cognitive demands (e.g., monitoring, supervising automated systems, planning, communicating and coordinating, and handling unanticipated situations). CTA methods provide a means to explicitly identify the knowledge and mental processing demands of cognitive work (e.g., what knowledge and skills people need to learn to do the job; what things they need to attend to and what mental calculations they must make to perform a task). CTA methods also provide a means to identify the kinds of errors that workers are prone to and the factors that contribute to those errors (e.g., confusable displays, high workload, lack of understanding of how the technology works).

Understanding the cognitive demands of work and the limitations of human performance is important when considering the introduction of new technology because it can help to define system requirements that will enable workers to perform well. For effective system design, it is as important to understand human performance limits as it is to understand the performance limits of the technology being considered. CTA methods can also be used to anticipate how the introduction of the technology is likely to impact the overall performance of the joint person-technology system. It is important to understand how people and technology will interact since these interactions represent emergent properties of the system that may not be apparent. For example, the introduction of a new PTC system that initiates automatic braking if the locomotive engineer approaches an end of authority too quickly may cause locomotive engineers to change their train operating behavior in unintended ways. Systems often produce behavior that would not be predicted by the behavior of the components. CTAs can be used to anticipate and address unintended side-effects of the introduction of new technology.

CTAs can inform all aspects of HSI starting from early system requirements exploration and definition through late stage validation and field testing. The results can be used to identify opportunities to improve performance either through the introduction of support systems that more effectively support cognitive performance (e.g., by integrating needed information in a single display that had previously been spread across multiple displays) or through training (e.g., to bring less experienced personnel to the level of experts). Cognitive analyses have also been used to guide other aspects of complex system analysis and design, including personnel selection, manning and function-allocation decisions, or as input to workload analysis and human reliability analysis.

A CTA involves two activities. The first is a *knowledge acquisition* activity to collect information about the demands of the domain, the skills and strategies that domain practitioners have developed to handle domain demands, and the performance problems and errors that can arise. The second is an *analysis* activity that involves interpretation, synthesis, and abstraction to draw generic conclusions from the information collected. While all CTA methods include both of these activities, some methods place more emphasis on one or the other (c.f., Bisantz and Roth, 2008).

A variety of specific techniques for CTA knowledge acquisition have been developed that draw on basic principles and methods of cognitive psychology (Ericsson and Simon, 1993; Hoffman, 1987; Potter et al., 2000; Cooke, 1994; Roth and Patterson, 2005):

- structured interview techniques such as the Applied CTA method (Militello and Hutton, 1998) and the Goal-Directed Task Analysis method (Endsley, Bolte and Jones, 2003);
- critical incident analysis methods that investigate actual incidents that have occurred in the past (Flanagan, 1954; Dekker; 2000), the most prominent example of which is the Critical Decision Method (Klein, Calderwood and MacGregor, 1989);
- cognitive field observation studies that examine performance in actual environments or in high fidelity simulators (Woods, 1993; Roth and Patterson, 2005; Chapter 5 of Woods and Hollnagel, 2006);
- 'think aloud' protocol analysis methods where domain practitioners are asked to 'think aloud' as they solve actual or simulated problems (e.g., Gray and Kirschenbaum, 2000);
- and simulated task methods where domain practitioners are observed as they solve analog problems under controlled conditions (Patterson, Roth and Woods, 2001).

Typically, CTAs rely on current domain practitioners as the primary knowledge source. However, that is not always possible. For example, when designing 'first of a kind' systems, there may be no current operational users to observe or interview. 'First of a kind' systems are systems that represent a substantial leap from existing ones with respect to the technologies they employ and the concept of operations they envision. They are sometimes referred to as 'futuristic' or 'revolutionary' systems (as opposed to evolutionary systems). Examples include envisioned Navy ships with multimission capabilities and dramatically reduced crew size (e.g, Bisantz et al., 2003), new nuclear power plant designs with completely digital compact control rooms (Roth, et al., 2001), and multiple heterogeneous unmanned vehicles intended to be supervised by a single operator (e.g., Nehme et al, 2006).

In those cases, CTA analysts may leverage other knowledge sources including stakeholders and developers of the new system who can provide insight into the goals, functions, and envisioned concept of operation for the system (c.f., Bisantz et al., 2003). CTA analysts can also draw insights by examining the cognitive demands associated with similar systems and operational environments (e.g., examining experiences in aviation to draw insights about future railroad operations), as well as by examining the cognitive complexities that arise with current legacy systems that are likely to apply equally to future systems (e.g., complexities that arise in current railroad operations that will continue to be relevant when new technologies are introduced).

There are several analytic CTA methods that are particularly well-suited for application to 'first of a kind' systems. These methods emphasize the kind of information to be gathered and how it should be represented to inform 'first of a kind' system design, rather than the particular knowledge acquisition method to be used. Examples include Cognitive Work Analysis (Vicente, 1999); Applied Cognitive Work Analysis (Elm, et al., 2003); Function-based CTA (Roth and Mumaw, 1995) and the hybrid CTA method (Nehme, et al., 2006). These analytic methods provide explicit guidance on defining the information and support requirements for 'first of a kind' systems.

In general, the particular set of CTA techniques selected will largely be dictated by the goals of the analysis and the pragmatics of the specific local conditions (e.g., access to domain practitioners and practicality of performing observations in the actual work environment). If the goal of the analysis is to gain a broad brush overview of cognitive and collaborative requirements and challenges in a domain so as to identify *leverage points* where new technology could have significant positive impact, then techniques such as field observations and structured interview techniques are very effective. If the goal is to develop detailed training curricula or to produce assessment protocols to establish practitioner proficiency (e.g., for accreditation purposes), then methods such as the Critical Decision Method and 'think aloud' verbal protocol that capture the detailed knowledge and skills (e.g., mental models, declarative and procedural knowledge) that distinguish practitioners at different levels of proficiency can be particularly useful. If the intent is to perform a 'moment by moment' analysis of monitoring and workload demands, then techniques such as 'eye-movement' analysis that capture performance at a more fine-grained level may be most appropriate. Finally, if the goal is to derive information and support requirements for a 'first of a kind' system, then analytic CTA methods that are explicitly designed for this purpose may be most appropriate.

The CTA methods selected will also be strongly influenced by the pragmatic constraints of the project, including time available and level of access to domain practitioners and the actual work environment. The CTA toolkit contains a variety of methods that can be tailored to the needs and constraints of the particular application. For example, if access to the actual work environment is not possible, thereby precluding the possibility of conducting field observations, then structured interview techniques can be used. If experts cannot discuss actual cases (e.g., because the information is classified or proprietary), then analyses can be conducted using simulated scenarios or analogous problems. If access to domain experts is not possible, it may be possible to conduct CTA based on review of documented descriptions of past critical incidents (e.g., accident reports).

FRA-sponsored CTAs of railroad workers have typically employed multiple converging methods; for example, structured interviews coupled with field observations. The structured interviews were often conducted in a focus group session, with several railroad workers being interviewed at the same time. A focus group interview approach was adopted to minimize the time demands placed on the host railroads, as well as to maximize data collection efficiency. Results from focus group interviews were generally complemented by observations of railroad workers in their actual work settings (i.e., field observations) so as to validate and extend the insights gained from the interviews. Typically, observations and interviews were conducted at multiple sites to include a representative range of types of railroads (e.g., passenger and freight; small and large) and geographic characteristics (e.g., flat and mountainous terrain) so as to assess the bounds of generality of the findings.

The output of a CTA can take multiple forms. Bisantz and Roth (2008) provide numerous examples of types of tabular and graphic representations that have been used to communicate the output of a CTA. In some cases, the output is a narrative description of critical incidents and the cognitive demands and strategies they reveal. It can also take the form of structured tables that catalogue the decision points that arise, why they are difficult, the knowledge and skill that enable experts to handle the situation, and the typical errors that less experienced personnel make. Other outputs produced from a CTA include concept maps that provide graphic depictions of the structure and knowledge content of domain practitioners (both experts and less experienced individuals) and diagrams that illustrate the problem-solving strategies used by domain practitioners (e.g., contrasting expert versus novice strategies). There are also graphic representations that provide explicit traceable links from cognitive analysis results to information, display, and support requirements.

With the FRA-sponsored CTAs, the primary purpose was to identify and document cognitively challenging aspects of the current work to anticipate potential impacts of new technologies on railroad worker performance. A related objective was to provide guidance for the design and introduction of those new technologies. The results of the CTAs and implications for introduction of new technology were documented as narrative descriptions and summary tables in FRA-sponsored CTA reports, cited in Section 1.

3.1   CONTRIBUTIONS TO SYSTEM DESIGN PHASES

CTA methods are increasingly being used to inform the introduction of new technology and to support the design of 'first of a kind' systems. A prominent example is the Cognitive Work Analysis (CWA) framework (Rasmussen, 1986; Rasmussen, Petersen, and Goodstein, 1994; Vicente, 1999). CWA uses a structured set of interlinked analyses as the foundation for deriving implications for system design, function allocation, team and organization structure, and training. Roth and Bisantz (2013) provide an overview of CWA and multiple examples of how it has been used to support system design. Empirical investigation of cognitive performance has also been used to inform design. Examples of ways that results from interviews and observations of current practitioners can be used to inform design include identifying strategies that suggest opportunities for redesign to improve performance (e.g., Crandall et al., 2006), identifying 'work-around' strategies that signal the need for more effective cognitive support (e.g., Mumaw, Roth, Vicente, and Burns, 2000), and identifying effective strategies that rely on features of the current environment that should be preserved or reproduced as new technology is introduced (e.g., Roth, Multer, and Raslear, 2006; Roth and Patterson, 2005). Examples of successful design applications that have relied on cognitive analysis include:

- redesign of the Airborne Warning and Control System (AWACS) weapons director station (Klinger and Gomes, 1993);
- design of next generation Navy ships (Bisantz et al., 2003; Burns, Bisantz, and Roth, 2004);

- design of next generation power plants (Roth, Lin, Kerch, Kenney, and Sugibayashi, 2001);
- design of auditory displays for anesthesia monitoring (Watson and Sanderson, 2007); and
- design of integrated visualizations for airlift mission planning and execution (Roth, Stilson et al., 2006).

CTAs have also been used to support development of training programs, performance evaluations, and analyses of contributors to human error, as well as to capture corporate knowledge (Crandall et al., 2006; Klein and Wolf, 1995; Naikar, 2006; Roth and Woods, 1988; Schaafstal, Schraagen and van Berlo, 2000). In addition, CWA techniques have been used to define team size and composition (Naikar, Pearce, Drumm and Sanderson, 2003) and evaluate competing design proposals for large system procurement (Naikar and Sanderson, 2001).

CTAs are particularly useful as part of early exploratory analyses in support of understanding needs and envisioning opportunities—what the National Academies of Science report referred to as 'defining opportunities and context of use' (NRC, 2007). They can be used to help focus further analyses and design efforts on those aspects of performance that are most cognitively challenging and error prone and identify *leverage points* where the introduction of new technology can have the most positive impact on performance. The output of CTA can also be used to define cognitively demanding scenarios and targets for effective performance that can inform design. The scenarios and performance targets can also be used in later evaluations of the effectiveness of the new design.

CTA methods continue to be relevant throughout the system development process, up to and including when systems are fielded. Context of use is constantly evolving, and introduction of new technology can produce operational and organizational changes, not all of which will have been anticipated ahead of time (Woods and Dekker, 2000; Patterson, Cook and Render, 2002; Roth et al., 2006). For example, as part of a power plant control room upgrade, computerized procedures were developed that integrated plant parameter information with the procedures so that the lead operator could work through the procedures without having to ask others for plant state information. This change had the (anticipated) consequence of improving the lead operator's situational awareness of plant state and the speed with which the procedures could be executed. However, it decreased the situational awareness of the other crew members (an unanticipated negative consequence) because the lead operator no longer needed to keep them as tightly in the loop. This unintended negative consequence was discovered during observational studies conducted as part of initial system introduction (O'Hara and Roth, 2005). As a consequence, crew operating philosophy and training were completely redefined to capitalize on the crew members' freed up mental resources (they could now provide an independent and diverse check on plant state) resulting in improved shared situational awareness for the entire team.

This example highlights the contributions that CTA can continue to provide up to and beyond system introduction to establish that the intended benefits of new technologies are realized and that unintended side effects (e.g., new forms of error; new vulnerabilities to risk) are identified and mitigated.

17

Below we summarize the different ways CTA can inform HSI in railroad operations:

Define the broader context of use within which a new technology will be deployed
CTAs can be useful in defining and understanding the range of contextual conditions, demands, and complexities that need to be considered in designing and evaluating new technologies. CTAs also help identify opportunities for more effective support; for example, they can help identify situations where new support, by way of new technology, additional crewmembers, or new processes, can make operations safer or more efficient. Additionally, CTAs help identify information and support requirements that the new technology needs to provide. In these ways, CTA can support HSI activities associated with deriving 'lessons learned' and guidance from operating experience review; it can also play a pivotal role in the requirements gathering phase of HSI.

Explore implications of introduction of new technology
CTA methods can also be used to understand how people and technology will interact and to identify unanticipated, emergent properties of the joint person-technology system. For example, the introduction of new technology has the potential to both remove tasks from the crew and create new tasks and responsibilities for them. CTAs can be performed during the early requirements definition and design development phases of HSI to identify those changes to crew tasks and responsibilities, as well as identify unanticipated side effects (e.g., new forms of error; new training requirements) that need to be avoided or addressed. CTAs can also be used in later phases of design and early field testing to support mid-course correction by looking for and addressing any additional unanticipated performance or safety issues that may arise. Finally, CTA can be used, post technology deployment, to continue to monitor for and address emergent issues.

Support HFE Analyses
Results of CTAs also feed into and inform a number of the human factors engineering analyses that are performed as part of HSI, including task analysis, workload analysis, function allocation analysis, staffing requirements, procedure and training, human reliability analysis, and design of validation studies. For example, CTA can help to identify knowledge and skill requirements that can instruct training development. It can complement traditional task analysis methods to identify information and decision-aiding requirements that support broad situational awareness and enhance the ability to respond in challenging, unanticipated situations. It can aid human reliability analyses by providing insight into ways new technology is likely to reduce some forms of errors as well as new forms of errors that may emerge. Cognitively challenging cases identified during CTAs can also help establish the range of representative situations and complicating factors that need to be embedded in evaluation scenarios and simulator-based tests to ensure that new technology will adequately support individual and team performance without introducing new sources of workload, unanticipated side effects, and opportunities for error. Finally, CTAs can identify human performance issues that require more focused investigation through prototyping, simulation, or experiments, for example.

Inform issues of concern

Finally, CTAs are often conducted to inform issues of concern. For example, there may be interest in understanding whether the introduction of a new technology affords the opportunity for crew reduction. A CTA can be used to better understand the various roles and responsibilities associated with each crew position to be able to assess which of those roles and responsibilities are eliminated (or taken on) by the new technology and which remain and must be accounted for in some other way if the crew position is eliminated. This example, and additional examples of how CTAs can inform HSI, can be found in the illustrative cases drawn from previous FRA-sponsored CTAs below.

3.2 ILLUSTRATIVE CASES DRAWN FROM FRA RESEARCH

In this section, we refer to four prior railroad worker CTAs that were conducted to provide concrete examples of ways CTA can inform design of new or existing systems. Examples are drawn from each of the CTAs to illustrate how results of CTAs can be used to inform different HSI domains (as defined in MANPRINT) as well as different HSI activities (as defined by the NRC).

Table 3 shows the six HSI domains relevant to the railroad industry and, in the rows beside each domain, the railroad worker CTAs whose key findings and recommendations informed that domain. Similarly, Table 4 shows the HSI activities and, in the rows beside each activity, the railroad worker CTAs whose key findings and recommendations informed that activity. A striking finding of this exercise is that across the four railroad CTAs, we were able to identify key CTA findings and recommendations of relevance to all of the MANPRINT domains and nearly all of the HSI activities defined by the NRC.

Table 3. HSI Domains* (as defined by the U.S. Army's MANPRINT) covered in CTA examples

HSI Domain	Railroad Worker CTA			
	Locomotive Engineer	Conductor	Dispatcher	Roadway Worker
Manpower	√	√		
Personnel			√	
Training	√	√	√	
Human Factors Engineering	√		√	√
System Safety & Health Hazards	√			√

*Soldier Survivability is not included in the table because it is not relevant to the railroad industry,

Table 4. HSI Activities (as defined by the NRC) covered in CTA examples

HSI Domain	Railroad Worker CTA			
	Locomotive Engineer	Conductor	Dispatcher	Roadway Worker
Operating Experience Review	√		√	√
Function Analysis & Allocation	√	√		√
Task Analysis*	√	√	√	√
Staffing & Qualifications			√	
Human Reliability Analysis	√			√
Human-System Interface Design	√		√	√
Procedure Development	√			
Training Program Development	√	√	√	
Verification & Validation				
Design Implementation	√			
Human Performance Monitoring				

*Though not a traditional task analysis, CTA is a type of task analysis, therefore all four CTAs are included in this row.

Sections 3.2.1–3.2.4, below, provide summaries for each of the four, FRA-sponsored CTAs used for this exercise. The associated tables (5–7) show how the type of information garnered from these CTAs can help inform the HSI process. The tables include information garnered from the CTAs, how the example informs the HSI process, and which domain (within the U.S. Army's MANPRINT program) and activity (within the NRC review criteria) the example fits under. More information about each CTA can be found in the FRA-published reports (see references).

3.2.1 Locomotive Engineer CTA

An important aim of the locomotive engineer CTA was to identify cognitive activities that could be supported more effectively through the introduction of advanced technologies, such as PTC, that are currently being developed by the railroad industry and evaluated as a part of FRA research and development efforts. A second related aim was to anticipate new cognitive demands and complexities that the new technologies might pose. While PTC technologies have the potential to improve the safety and efficiency of railroad operations, they also have the potential to create new failure modes and impose new cognitive demands on locomotive engineers who need to monitor PTC displays and provide inputs to the system. Part of the purpose of the CTA was to understand these potential new performance demands.

The locomotive engineer CTA was based on an extensive series of interviews and observations that were made at seven sites between February 2000 and September 2005. These sites included both intercity passenger operations, commuter operations, and freight operations. Five of the sites were at locations where railroads were in the process of field testing advanced train control technologies. PTC systems we examined included:

- Computer-Based Train Management (CBTM)
- Advanced Speed Enforcement System (ASES)
- Incremental Train Control System (ITCS)
- Electronic Train Management System (ETMS)
- North American Joint Positive Train Control (NAJPTC)

The results of the CTAs were documented in a series of FRA reports including Wreathall, Roth, Bley and Multer, 2007; and Roth and Multer, 2008.

The CTA identified the major cognitive functions that underlie locomotive engineer performance and the factors that contribute to cognitive challenges. Important cognitive functions include the need to maintain broad situational awareness and develop an accurate current situation model of the immediate environment (including the location, activities, and intentions of other agents such as other trains and roadway workers in the vicinity); the need to generate expectations and think ahead to know where to focus attention, prepare for anticipated actions, and plan for contingencies; the need to actively engage in sustained visual and auditory monitoring (e.g., monitoring radio communication); the need to manage multiple demands on attention; the need to prioritize and manage multiple goals; and the need for rapid decision making in response to unanticipated conditions (e.g., a person or object obstructing the track).

The interviews and observations conducted at sites where new train control technologies were being introduced revealed that while these new technologies reduced some cognitive demands (e.g., some systems reduce memory demands by presenting work zone locations and temporary speed restrictions on in-cab displays), they also created new ones. These new cognitive demands, in turn, can lead to changes in how locomotive engineers operate the train. Sources of new cognitive demands included:

- Constraints imposed by the PTC braking profile that require locomotive engineers to modify train handling strategies;
- Increases in information and alerts provided by the in-cab displays that require locomotive engineers to focus more attention on in-cab displays as opposed to out the window;
- Requirements for extensive interaction with the PTC systems (e.g., to initialize it; to acknowledge messages and alerts) that impose new sources of workload; and
- Conflicts between attentional demands inside the locomotive cab with respect to managing train control and attentional demands outside the locomotive cab from hazards such as trespassers, motor vehicles approaching grade crossings, and objects fouling the track.

The locomotive engineer CTA report concluded that while PTC technology is likely to have a positive impact on overall risk of accidents, the new sources of cognitive demands associated with PTC have the potential to contribute to new forms of errors and accidents (c.f., Wreathall et al., 2007a, b). Careful consideration of these new sources of cognitive demand is needed during the HSI process to ensure that the design of the PTC automation and in-cab displays, as well as the development of accompanying training processes and procedures minimize the potential for new sources of error and accidents.

Table 5 summarizes some of the insights that can be drawn from the locomotive engineer CTA that are of relevance to the different domains and activities of the HSI process. This table provides an illustration of how a CTA can be used to inform HSI. Fuller descriptions are provided in the locomotive engineer CTA report (Roth and Multer, 2008) and another FRA sponsored report summarizing human factors considerations in the evaluation of processor-based signal and train control systems (Wreathall et al., 2007b) .

Table 5. Examples drawn from locomotive engineer CTA (DOT/FRA/ORD-09/03)

Domain/HSI Activity	How example informs the HSI process	CTA Finding/Recommendation
Domain: HFE (Activity: Operating Experience Review)	• Explore implications of introduction of new technology • Identify opportunities for more effective support	**Improved Anticipation:** PTC systems that provide preview information such as upcoming speed restrictions (both permanent and temporary speed restrictions); location of workzones; location and velocity of nearby traffic; and upcoming distance cues (e.g., mileposts, switches and stations) as part of in-cab displays reduce memory demands on locomotive engineers, foster a more accurate situation model, and make it easier for locomotive engineers to generate expectations and prepare for upcoming conditions.
Domain: HFE (Activity: Operating Experience Review)	• Explore implications of introduction of new technology • Identify additional tasks (or changes to tasks)	**New Cognitive Tasks or Changes to Cognitive Tasks:** • *Impact on train handling strategies:* constraints imposed by the PTC braking profile require locomotive engineers to modify their previously learned train handling strategies • *Impact on attention allocation and monitoring:* increases in information and alerts provided by the in-cab displays require locomotive engineers to focus more attention on in-cab displays as opposed to out the window
Domain: System Safety (Activity: Human Reliability Analysis)	• Explore implications of introduction of new technology • Identify impact on system safety and health hazards • Identify unanticipated side effects and potential	**Potential for Complacency:** There is the potential for train crews to become overly reliant on the new train control technologies (complacency). Locomotive engineers may come to rely on the PTC system to alert them of upcoming speed and authority limits and to automatically stop the train should they fail to do so themselves. If the system fails, the locomotive engineers may not perform as well without it as they would have had the system never been installed. Concerns include

	negative consequences	that the train crew may not realize or may forget that the PTC system has failed (or is off) and is thus no longer providing the level of support they are expecting; concern that the train crew may be delayed in detecting and responding to PTC system failures; and concern that the crew may lose skill due to lack of practice, and thus may not be able to perform tasks as well when the system is not available. **Interoperability Issues:** The movement of crews from equipped to unequipped trains, or territory where PTC support is not available can potentially make it possible for crews to forget that the PTC system is no longer available. **New Risk Associated with Inadvertent Activation of Penalty Break:** If the PTC braking profile is conservative, it may require the locomotive crew to learn new train handling and braking techniques to avoid unnecessary PTC penalty brake application while still operating efficiently. A concern, particularly for inexperienced crews, is the possibility of inadvertent activation of a penalty brake that creates risk (e.g., train stops at inappropriate location or train derails). **Integration with Existing Systems:** Multiple cab displays may provide conflicting information, or the same information in multiple forms. This may create opportunity for error, particularly in the case of new engineers or those who only use these systems occasionally.
Domain: Manpower (Activity: Functional Analysis & Allocation)	• Explore implications of introduction of new technology • Identify or uncover additional issues and considerations	**Impact on Teamwork Processes:** Depending on design, the PTC system could potentially alter established train crew teamwork practices, particularly if the PTC display is placed in a location so that only the locomotive engineer can see the display, thereby reducing the ability of the second individual in the cab to provide a redundancy check. For example, train crews may lose shared understanding of current situation with the technology if its actions are not transparent or the technology may not understand what the train crew is doing due to lack of communication.
Domain: HFE (Activity: Human-	• Support HFE Analyses • Identify information and	**Implications for In-Cab Display Requirements:** • There is a need for improved in-cab displays

System Interface Design, Procedure Development)	support requirements that can inform design of the new technology • Identify procedure requirements resulting from new technology	that minimize the need to visually attend to the in-cab display to extract important information. Specifically, there is a need for in-cab displays that make it easier to anticipate and stay within the braking curve without having to look closely at the in-cab display so that more attention can be allocated to looking outside the window.
		• Multiple instances were documented where PTC could initiate an automatic penalty brake inappropriately. Procedures need to be put into place that will allow locomotive engineers mechanisms and authority to suppress an automatic penalty brake under conditions where it is inappropriate and potentially a safety hazard.
Domain: Training (Activity: Training Program Development)	• Support HFE Analyses	**Implications for Training:** • In-class training is needed to understand how the PTC system works (technical theory). • In-class and hands-on training is needed to understand how to operate the PTC system under different conditions (e.g., how to initialize it, what the different PTC displays mean, what error modes might arise, and what to do in those different conditions) and the applicable book of operating rules (PTC operations). • Hands-on experience or simulator training is required to learn the new train handling and braking strategies required to operate a PTC-equipped train efficiently while staying within the PTC braking profile (hands-on train handling). • Hands-on experience or simulator training is required to reduce the attention demands associated with monitoring in-cab displays. A substantial learning curve exists to reach the point where the in-cab display does not serve as a source of distraction, diverting attention away from events out the window. Locomotive engineers must have sufficient experience in running a PTC-equipped train as part of training so that they get beyond the point where close monitoring of the in-cab display is required to avoid a penalty brake application.

		Alternatively, there needs to be a strategy for how to allocate attention between activities inside and outside the locomotive cab. • Hands-on experience is also needed to learn how to handle the 'traps', challenging situations, and failure conditions that are known to arise in special circumstances (rare events). • Continued training and experience running the trains without the PTC system on (or with selective portions of the PTC in-cab display off) to maintain skill so that if the system ever fails the engineer will still be able to operate the train safely.
Domain: HFE (Activity: Verification & Validation)	• Support HFE Analyses • Specify range of representative situations and complicating factors that need to be embedded in evaluation scenarios and simulator-based tests	**Range of Special Conditions to Include in a Person-in-the-Loop Evaluation:** Challenging situations that can arise that need to be represented in an evaluation include: • traveling on a steep uphill grade with a fully loaded train and suddenly coming upon a PTC enforcement target location • operating a PTC train with inaccurate consist information • operating a PTC train where the PTC system fails at some point during the trip • operating a track where PTC fails or the system lacks PTC • operating over territory where multiple forms of PTC exist that work differently from one another and require the train crew to operate the train differently under similar conditions.
Domain: HFE (Activity: Human-System Interface Design)	• Support HFE analyses • Identify areas where more focused investigation is required (via prototyping, simulation, or experiments)	**Need to Minimize In-Cab Visual Attention Demands:** There is a need for in-cab displays that minimize the need to visually attend to the in-cab display to extract important information. It would be desirable to develop alternative display approaches for indicating to the locomotive engineer where train speed is in relation to the desired deceleration rate without having to closely

		monitor the visual in-cab display. Options to explore include the use of nonvisual display modes such as auditory or tactile displays. Heads-up displays that would allow users to track critical driving parameters while still looking out the cab may provide an alternative promising research direction.

3.2.2 Freight Conductor CTA

In addition to understanding the role of the train conductor in freight rail operation, an important objective of the conductor CTA was to understand the implications of the Rail Safety Improvement Act (RSIA) of 2008 on the role of the conductor, specifically with regard to the mandate for conductor certification and implementation of PTC on applicable freight and passenger rail lines. The goal was to understand conductor training programs currently in place, as well as upcoming training trends, to provide insight to FRA for the conductor certification effort and, to the extent possible, understand and anticipate potential impacts of PTC on the conductor's work.

The CTA was based on interviews, focus groups, and site visits conducted between January 2009 and April 2010. A total of 23 stakeholders, railroad practitioners, experienced conductors, conductor trainers, and training managers were interviewed from:

- Federal Railroad Administration (FRA),
- American Association of Railroads (AAR),
- United Transportation Union (UTU),
- Transportation Technology Center, Inc. (TTCI),
- National Academy of Railroad Sciences (NARS),
- Burlington Northern Santa Fe (BNSF),
- and Union Pacific Railroad (UP).

Site visits included a trip to the NARS facility, the UP Beaumont Yard, and the UP Houston Yard. Results from the CTA can be found in a Human Factors and Ergonomics Society paper (Rosenhand and Roth, 2011) and an FRA report (Rosenhand, Roth and Multer, 2012).

The CTA identified cognitive tasks and associated challenges of freight train conductor work, specified key findings with respect to implementation of PTC and conductor certification, and pointed out future research needs.

One of the questions that motivated the CTA was how new technologies such as PTC are likely to impact the role of conductors in the future. The CTA addressed this issue by laying out the multiple ways in which conductors contribute to safe and efficient train operations and contrasting these with anticipated features of positive train control. Results of the CTA show that an important role conductors serve is in handling unanticipated events, which include a variety of situations where conductors are required to troubleshoot the source of the problem and take appropriate action. Another finding points to the importance of conductors in supporting the locomotive engineer; for example, by monitoring the outside environment through the cab window for potential obstacles and hazards that would not be detected by automated systems and filling in knowledge gaps that locomotive engineers may have (particularly less experienced engineers). Finally, conductors also serve an important role in keeping the locomotive engineer alert (and vice versa) on long monotonous trips where there is a risk of falling asleep. These findings supported the conclusion that PTC will not account for all of the cognitive and physical support functions that conductors currently provide.

In addition to understanding how PTC is likely to impact the role of conductors, the CTA also sought to uncover implications for conductor training. Interviews from the CTA revealed the importance of territory familiarization and experience in the field. Conductors stressed the importance of knowledge of the territory, practicing routine skills, and having direct, hands-on experience performing tasks. Results suggest that by providing a broad set of carefully selected experiences as part of OJT, new conductors could potentially accelerate the building of expertise.

Additionally, conductors stressed the importance of effective cab communication and job briefing skills, particularly in situations where less experienced conductors are paired with more experienced locomotive engineers and the less experienced conductor may feel uncomfortable pointing out unsafe behavior. Interviews suggested that these skills are not always explicitly taught and not sufficiently stressed during training. Therefore, a focus on effective communication and increased crew resource management training would enhance teamwork and encourage joint problem-solving and decision making that could leverage the knowledge and skills of the entire train crew. Finally, results from the CTA point to the value of carefully pairing conductors and locomotive engineers so that less experienced individuals are paired with more experienced ones. This not only makes for a safer and more efficient train crew, it also provides opportunities for knowledge transfer between crew members, further accelerating development of expertise.

Table 6 illustrates how a CTA can inform HSI. Additional information and more detailed CTA results can be found in the FRA-sponsored Conductor CTA report (Rosenhand, Roth and Multer, 2012).

Table 6. Examples drawn from Freight Train Conductor CTA (DOT/FRA/ORD-12/13)

Domain/HSI Activity	How example informs the HSI process	CTA Findings and Recommendations
Domain: Manpower (Activity: Function Analysis & Allocation)	• Inform issues of concern (e.g., one vs. two person operation) • Support HFE analyses • Identify additional tasks that would result from the introduction of the new technology that would need	**It is not clear how the introduction of PTC will affect cognitive and collaborative processes, but findings suggest that it will not account for all the cognitive and physical support functions the conductor currently provides.** When installed as an overlay system, the train crew's current roles and responsibilities will not change, therefore it is not clear if or how train crew cognitive and collaborative processes will be affected. Simulator

		studies may help researchers understand the impact of PTC on railroad operations.
	• Identify information and support requirements that can inform design of the new technology.	Additionally, findings from the CTA suggest that positive train control technology will not account for all of the cognitive and physical support functions that the conductor currently provides, primarily with regard to:
		• Handling unanticipated events Conductors serve an important role in handling unanticipated events. These events include a variety of situations where conductors need to troubleshoot the source of the problem and take appropriate action. • Supporting the locomotive engineer Conductors support the locomotive engineer in monitoring the outside environment through the cab window for potential obstacles and hazards that would not be detected by automated systems, filling in knowledge gaps that locomotive engineers may have, and supporting decision making. • Keeping the locomotive engineer alert Conductors and locomotive engineers serve to keep each other alert, primarily during long, monotonous trips during which there is a risk of falling asleep. A subsequent job and cognitive task analysis would need to be conducted in order to identify new knowledge, skills, abilities, and other characteristics (KSAOs) required by the locomotive engineer if operations changed such that trains were operated by a one-person crew.
Domain : Training (Activity: Training Program Development)	• Support HFE analyses • Identify knowledge, skill, and training requirements	**Implications for Training:** • On-the-job training (OJT) is needed for rare but serious events. Providing a broader set of carefully selected experiences during OJT will enable conductors to more quickly build up their knowledge of the territory and gain direct experiences with a variety of situations. • Teaching conductors and locomotive engineers

| | | effective cab communication and job briefing skills will enhance teamwork and encourage joint problem-solving and decision making that leverages the knowledge and skills of the entire train crew. This goal can be supported by Crew Resource Management (CRM) training. |
| | | • Carefully pairing conductors and locomotive engineers so that less experienced individuals are paired with more experienced ones will make for a safer and more efficient train crew while providing opportunities for knowledge transfer between crew members. |

3.2.3 Dispatcher CTA

One of the main objectives of the dispatcher CTA was to examine how experienced dispatchers managed and scheduled trains when the study was conducted. The intent was to identify cognitive activities that could be supported more effectively through the introduction of new technology, and determine what features of the existing environment that contribute to effective performance needed to be preserved when transitioning to new technologies. At the time the CTA was conducted (1998), digital communications technology was emerging as a way to transfer information from the radio to a visual medium such as a computer display. An explicit goal of the CTA was to provide recommendations for how the data link technology could be deployed to improve communication efficiency and effectiveness; this was achieved by examining how voice radio communication was being used in its current environment. A secondary goal of the CTA was to make recommendations for potential improvements to dispatcher selection, training, and display and decision-support.

The CTA consisted of four phases, each building on the prior phase's results. Phase 1 involved 2 days of observing dispatchers as they went about their job in an Amtrak dispatch center in Boston that primarily handled passenger trains. Phase 2 consisted of structured interviews with experienced dispatchers and related personnel from the dispatch center where the first field observations were held. Topics covered included complicating factors that made track management and train routing difficult; the strategies that they have developed to facilitate performance and maintain the 'big picture'; issues in training new dispatchers; and suggestions for improved communication systems and computerized support systems. Phase 3 involved field observations at a second dispatch center that primarily handled freight trains (Conrail dispatch center in Pittsburgh, PA). The objective of this phase was to assess the generality of the results obtained at the first dispatch center. The fourth phase involved a second set of field observations at the Phase 1 dispatch center. The objective was to verify and expand on the results obtained in the previous three phases.

Results from the CTA reveal that dispatching is a complex, cognitively demanding task. Successful performance depends on the ability of dispatchers to monitor train movement beyond their territory, anticipate delays, balance multiple demands placed on track use, and make rapid decisions. To do this successfully, they must keep track of where trains are, whether they will reach their destination points on time or will be delayed, and how long the delays will be. Adding to the complexity of the job are the heavy attention and communication demands placed on dispatchers, who may be called on to monitor multiple activities in different parts of the territory at a time. The CTA revealed that displays in the dispatch centers did not provide the needed information for effective performance. The CTA documented a number of strategies that experienced dispatchers have developed to enable more efficient performance. A key finding of the CTA was that many of these strategies relied on the 'party-line' nature of radio communication which allowed dispatchers to extract needed information by 'listening in' to communication directed at others.

Results from the CTA pointed to suggestions for how new information, visualizations, and decision aids could be used to support dispatcher decision making. For example, more accurate information on train location and train movement would be useful, as would making things like operating rules, train timetables, speed bulletins, and policy updates, among others, available electronically for easier accessibility. Finally, results showed that displays providing accurate visualizations of the track and surrounding streets were beneficial to dispatchers, as were displays showing the location of personnel working on the track.

Another important finding of the CTA was related to the challenges and benefits of radio communication. Interviews and observations confirmed that voice radio channels were overloaded and congested. Further, the CTA revealed that voice radio was not well suited to some of the types of communication that were being conducted on it (e.g., complicated movement authorities with detailed time and location information). However, the CTA revealed that although the "party-line" voice radio communication was often noisy and congested, the 'broadcast' nature of radio communication provided a shared frame of reference that enabled dispatchers and others working on the railroad to anticipate situations and act proactively. Dispatchers reported that they routinely listened in for information on the radio channel that, although not addressed directly to them, alerted them to potential delays, problems, or calls for assistance. The CTA further concluded that any new communication system—data link, for example—would need to preserve the kind of information provided by the party line (information that was determined to be critical to safety and productivity). This finding didn't imply that 'party-line' voice radio needed to be preserved 'as is', but, rather, that the support functions it provided needed to be retained.

To reconcile these findings, the CTA sought to identify ways to deploy new technologies and still preserve the party-line aspect of voice communication. The CTA found that messages involving detailed instruction and precise location information were best communicated on data link (with information presented visually) through a private channel. However, messages that involved alerts about hazards on the track were better communicated on a broadcast channel to efficiently reach the most number of individuals. Accordingly, the CTA report offered specific guidance for the design of data link systems.

The dispatcher CTA results also revealed implications for dispatcher selection and training. The CTA found that dispatcher tasks required visual-spatial reasoning and spatial manipulation. The

CTA therefore determined that developing objective tests that require potential dispatchers to project train movement in time and space and visualize where work is to be conducted on the track (in conjunction with interviews) could possibly result in an improved selection process. Additionally, the CTA concluded that simulator-based training could possibly augment dispatcher apprenticeship training to bring new trainees up to a high level of performance. Examples of the types of skills that may be developed by simulator training can be found in Table 7 below.

Table 7. Examples drawn from dispatcher CTA (DOT/FRA/ORD-01/02)

Domain/HSI Activity	How example informs the HSI process	CTA Finding and Recommendation
Domain: HFE (Activity: Operating Experience Review)	• Define the broader context of use. Identify opportunities for more effective support. • Identify information and support requirements that can inform new technology design.	**Implications for Advanced Displays and Decision Aids:** • More accurate information on train location and train movement would be useful to better anticipate train delays and manage track more efficiently. • Shifting paper resources to electronic media will make referring to documents easier and better support dispatch decisions. • Providing dispatchers with more accurate visualizations of the physical track and surrounding geography will be useful and will help maintain the safety of personnel working on the track and enable dispatchers to effectively coordinate response in emergencies. • Decision aids that can help dispatchers manage unplanned events more effectively would be very useful.
Domain: HFE (Activity: Human-System Interface Design)	• Explore implications of introduction of new technology. • Identify unanticipated side effects and potential negative consequences.	**Data Link Technology:** Voice radio channels are overloaded and congested, and voice radio is not well suited to some of the types of communication that are now conducted on it. Therefore, there is a need to off-load communication onto other media, for example, data link technology. Data link technology allows for information to be transferred over data link instead of voice radio. Suggestions for data link technology use are as follows: • Data link should supplement (not supplant) voice

		<u>radio.</u> • <u>Mode presentation should depend on the nature of communication.</u> Messages involving detailed instruction and precise location information are best communicated via private channel with the information presented visually, whereas messages that involve alerts to hazards on the track are more appropriately communicated on a broadcast channel. • <u>Cognitive and collaborative tasks supported by the radio party-line should continue to be supported.</u> Shared graphic displays may help ensure that the party-line aspect of voice radio is not lost. They can reduce the potential for misunderstandings and communication errors.
Domain: Personnel (Activity: Staffing & Qualifications)	• Support HFE Analyses • Identify relevant aptitudes and experiences	**Implications for Dispatcher Crew Selection:** Current dispatcher selection relies primarily on interviews. Developing objective tests that can be used in combination with interviews may result in an improved selection process. Dispatching requires visual-spatial reasoning and spatial manipulation, therefore, tests that tap into this type of reasoning and correlate well with other aspects of dispatch performance may improve the selection process. More research would be needed to explore the link, if any, between spatial reasoning and dispatch performance, and the results could be used to develop a predictive test.
Domain: Training (Activity: Training Program Development)	• Support HFE Analyses • Identify knowledge, skill, and training requirements	**Implications for Dispatcher Training:** It may be possible to accelerate new hire learning through exposure to training scenarios in a simulator. Simulator-based training can augment apprenticeship and help to more quickly bring new trainees up to a high level of performance. Examples of skills that may benefit from simulator training include: • Strategies to support anticipation • Strategies to maintain broad awareness • Cooperative strategies to maximize route efficiency • Strategies for anticipating problems and planning contingencies • Strategies for leveling workload • Strategies for performing multiple tasks in parallel

3.2.4 Roadway Worker CTA

An important aim of the roadway worker CTA was to identify cognitive activities that could be supported more effectively through the introduction of advanced technologies such as PTC and portable digital communication devices that were being developed by the railroad industry (supported by FRA research and development programs). A second, related aim was to anticipate the impact of these new technologies on roadway workers, both in terms of new demands for equipment troubleshooting and maintenance and impact on roadway worker safety.

The research team performed interviews and observations in passenger and freight territories with the following crafts:

- 13 trackmen who are responsible for inspection and maintenance of the track;
- 8 signalmen who are responsible for inspection and maintenance of the signal systems; and
- 5 dispatchers who control track usage.

Interviews were conducted individually or in groups of up to five people at six railroad sites around the country.

Interview topics included the factors that impact roadway worker safety; the need for communication and coordination between dispatchers, train crews, and other roadway workers; the challenges that arise in performing inspection and maintenance tasks; and how new technologies, such as PTC and portable digital-based communication devices, might impact worker performance and safety.

The CTA identified cognitive and collaborative demands associated with roadway worker tasks, which primarily include work on and around the track, as well as track inspection, maintenance, and troubleshooting activities. Interviews and observations revealed that communication between roadway workers in one location, as well as among other railroad workers dispersed in space and time, plays a significant role in enabling the completion of tasks and creating safe working conditions. While many of these communications are mandated by formal operating rules, others are more informal—often described as courtesies—and serve to foster shared situational awareness and create safety nets for roadway workers.

The CTA uncovered many of these informal cooperative communication strategies, which include dispatchers alerting one another of approaching (particularly unscheduled) trains, coordinating with one another to aid roadway workers, and employees in charge monitoring radio communication to get a sense for train and roadway worker locations. Interviews revealed a number of instances where these informal cooperative strategies enabled errors to be caught and recovered from before severe consequences resulted. The CTA concluded that it is important to recognize the existence and value of these informal cooperative strategies to guide the design of more effective support systems and ensure that the introduction of new technology does not inadvertently disrupt informal communication and coordination processes that contribute to overall system safety.

To understand opportunities to enhance roadway worker performance and on-track safety through the use of digital communications, researchers looked at the use of portable digital communication systems and PTC technology. The CTA found that portable digital communication systems that combine location information with digital communication have the potential to facilitate communication and coordination among roadway workers, dispatchers, and locomotive engineers and enhance safety. Possible benefits of such a system include, for example, the ability to obtain and release working limits more efficiently, more reliable communication and reduced potential for communication errors, and opportunities to warn roadway workers of approaching trains. Section 3.4.2 of DOT/FRA/ORD-07/28 identified specific support function requirements of portable digital communication devices based on the results of analysis of roadway worker cognitive and collaborative demands.

The results of the CTA reaffirmed the potential benefits of PTC technology for enhancing roadway worker safety. PTC systems have been explicitly designed to stop trains before they enter work zones, which protect roadway workers from trains exceeding their limits of authority due to train crew error or communication failures. PTC technology, coupled with digital communication technology, can also enhance roadway worker safety outside work zones by providing roadway workers with accurate information as to the location and movement of trains in their vicinity and alerts when trains are approaching their location.

Finally, in addition to pointing out opportunities to enhance roadway worker performance through the use of digital communication technologies, the results of the CTA also revealed a need for more effective support for maintenance activities. This includes explicit consideration of system maintainability during the design phase, more training (including refresher training), better manuals, better self-diagnostics, and more technical support from vendors. The need for more effective support will become increasingly important as new, advanced digital systems requiring different knowledge and skills to troubleshoot and maintain are introduced.

Table 8. Examples drawn from roadway worker CTA (DOT/FRA/ORD-07/28)

Domain and HSI Activity	How example informs the HSI process	CTA Finding and Recommendation
Domain: HFE (Activity: Operating Experience Review; Human-System Interface Design)	• Explore implications of introduction of new technology. • Identify opportunities for more effective support. • Identify information and support requirements that the new technology needs to meet.	**Portable Roadway Worker Devices Have Potential to Facilitate Communication and Enhance Situation Awareness:** Portable roadway worker devices that can combine more accurate location information technology with more reliable communication technology have the potential to facilitate communication and coordination among roadway workers, dispatchers, and locomotive engineers. By incorporating broadcast capabilities that enable messages to be sent to multiple individuals at the same time, it is possible to preserve some of the positive party-line aspects of analog radio communication that foster shared situational awareness of the locations and

		activities of others working in the same vicinity.
		Section 3.4.2 listed specific support functions that could be provided by a portable communication device to support the cognitive and collaborative demands of roadway workers.
		Potential Benefits Include:
		• Ability to obtain and release working limits more efficiently (e.g., through reduction in failed attempts to reach a party due to radio congestion, dead zones, etc.)
		• More reliable communication and reduced potential for communication errors
		• Opportunity to warn roadway workers when they are about to exceed their limits of authority (either going outside geographic limits, working on the wrong track, or approaching time expiration)
		• Opportunity to warn roadway workers of approaching trains (both on the track they may be working on or near and on adjacent tracks)
		• Improved ability to keep track of and coordinate with other roadway workers in a work group
		• Improved ability to maintain awareness of trains in the vicinity
		• Improved ability for dispatchers to maintain situational awareness of the location and dispersion of roadway workers and equipment in their territories
Domain: HFE (Activity: Operating Experience Review)	• Explore implications of introduction of new technology. • Identify opportunities for more effective support.	**Use of PTC Technology to Enhance Roadway Worker Safety** • PTC will protect roadway workers from trains exceeding their limits of authority as a result of train crew error or communication failures. • PTC, coupled with digital communication technology, can also enhance roadway worker safety outside working limits by providing them with accurate information as to the location and movement of trains in their vicinity and alert them when trains are approaching their location.

Domain: HFE (Activity: Operating Experience Review; Design Implementation;)	• Explore implications of introduction of new technology. • Identify unanticipated side effects of introduction that need to be addressed. • Identify/uncover additional issues/considerations.	**Design New Technology for Maintainability:** As new systems are developed, it is important to consider issues of maintainability as part of the system design and evaluation process. Additionally, there is a need for more effective support for maintenance activities, including training (and refresher training), better manuals, better self-diagnostics, and more technical support from vendors. The need for more effective support is particularly important as new, advanced digital systems which require different knowledge and skills to troubleshoot and maintain are introduced.
Domain: System Safety and Health Hazards; HFE (Activity: Operating Experience Review; Human Reliability Analysis)	• Define the broader context of use within which a new technology will be deployed • Define the range of contextual conditions, demands, and complexities that need to be considered in designing and evaluating new technologies. • Identify impact on system safety and health hazards	**Cross-Craft Cooperative Strategies for Facilitating Work and Enhancing Safety:** Communication and coordination among multiple individuals engaged in different roadway tasks and dispersed across locations is important for facilitating work and enhancing safety. Roadway workers, dispatchers, and train crews have developed informal cooperative strategies that contribute to the overall safety of railroad operations. Though these strategies are not codified in operating rules and are often described as courtesies, they serve to foster shared situational awareness and create safety nets. These informal cooperative strategies should be recognized and valued and should guide the design of more effective support systems; this will ensure that the introduction of new technology does not inadvertently disrupt existing informal communication channels and coordination processes that contribute to overall system safety.

3.3 ADDITIONAL CTA APPROACHES TO INFORM HSI IN THE RAILROAD INDUSTRY

The FRA-sponsored railroad worker CTAs aimed to provide a clear picture of the contextual factors that impact performance and the cognitive and collaborative strategies that domain practitioners have developed in response to work demands. As mentioned earlier, this type of analysis can guide development and deployment of new technology.

There are other CTA methods that can be used to provide more fine-grained input to HSI analysis and design activities. For example, there are CTA methods that provide a more detailed, second-by-second description of the mental processes (e.g., perceptual processes, attention processes, memory store and retrieval processes) involved in performing complex cognitive tasks such as running a train. These more microcognitive-level analyses can be particularly helpful for analyzing attention and workload demands at an in-depth level.

There have been a number of recent attempts to examine the microlevel (second by second) information processing involved in operating the train over a route. Examples include Luke, Brook-Carter, Parkes, Grimes, and Mills (2006) who employed eye tracking recordings to analyze the detailed visual scanning strategies used by locomotive engineers; Jansson, Olsson, and Erlandsson (2006) who used think-aloud protocols to examine the moment-by-moment attention and thinking processes as locomotive engineers drove a train route; Gillis (2005) who examined the detailed serial and parallel mental processes and how they varied over the time course of a train trip; and Hamilton and Clarke (2005) who developed a computational model intended to predict locomotive engineer workload and performance time for different routes. These microlevel CTA methods complement the more high-level cognitive analyses methods that were used in the FRA CTA.

Analytic CTA methods intended to derive information and support requirements for 'first of a kind' systems are also of relevance to the railroad industry. Methods such as Cognitive Work Analysis (Vicente, 1999), Applied Cognitive Work Analysis (Elm, et al., 2003), and the hybrid CTA (Nehme, et al., 2006) would be useful for providing traceable links explicitly showing how features of future human-system interfaces would support challenging cognitive tasks. One example that has been used in the railroad industry is the hybrid CTA method (Nehme et al., 2006). Tappan and colleagues (Tappan, Pittman, Abi Akar, and Cummings, 2011) used a hybrid CTA to generate requirements for a prototype planning and scheduling display that provides real-time feedback to train drivers to help them maintain on-time train operation and adhere to the published train schedule. The hybrid CTA method was used to identify information and functional requirements for the prototype display, including information requirements needed to support situational awareness.

Which type of CTA to use depends on the particular point in the HSI process, the goals of the analysis, and the nature of the analysis questions to be answered.

3.4 LESSONS LEARNED ACROSS THE RAILWAY WORKER CTAS

One of the striking findings of the review of the four railway worker CTAs is that they yielded insights across all the HSI domains. Those insights can potentially inform personnel selection, manpower (staffing level) requirements, training, technology design, and system safety analysis. The review yielded examples of how CTAs can be used in support of virtually all the activities that fall under the HSI umbrella including: operating experience review, function analysis and allocation, task analysis, staffing and qualifications, human reliability analysis, human-system interface design, training program development, and verification and validation. The only notable exception was human performance monitoring, for which there were no CTA-generated examples because the CTAs were conducted prior to the introduction of the new technology and not after it was fielded. There were, however, examples of CTA use to support operator experience review, which is on the same continuum as human performance monitoring.

The CTAs illustrated how examination of performance in the current environment could be used to identify opportunities to improve performance using new technologies; they also provided guidance on how to design those new technologies so as to avoid unanticipated negative consequences. Perhaps the best example was the dispatcher CTA that explored both the drawbacks and benefits of 'party-line' radio communication to inform design of digital communication technologies that eliminated the negative features of radio communication while preserving some of the positive features of 'party-line' broadcast communication.

The CTAs also highlighted the importance of exploring the potential impact of proposed new technologies on worker performance. Both the locomotive and conductor CTAs drew on experiences with early versions of PTC systems to identify human performance issues that needed to be addressed. Addressing those issues involved identifying new cognitive demands, new needs for training, and new potential sources of risk. Making PTC system developers and regulators aware early on of potential performance and safety concerns ensures that the issues are recognized and properly addressed as part of the design process.

In summary, the review of CTAs provided concrete illustration of how CTAs can be used to:

- Identify cognitive and collaborative activities that can benefit from more effective support;
- Identify the kinds of aid that would be most effective (e.g., the types of information needed and how the information can best be presented);
- Identify design pitfalls to avoid (e.g., potential negative side effects, or new cognitive and collaborative demands associated with the new technology that need to be addressed);
- Mitigate the risk of design failures by promoting a more complete understanding of needs and design challenges;
- Guide mid-course design corrections that lay the groundwork for next-generation system development.

4. EMERGING HSI ISSUES IN THE RAILROAD INDUSTRY

Railroad operations in the United States are undergoing rapid changes, many of which are related to the implementation of new technologies. FRA introduced HSI to the railroad industry (Reinach and Jones, 2007) as a way to help with acquisition of new technology. Creating an HSI framework that can be used by railroads for technology acquisition processes will help reduce potential mismatches between the technology and human operator limitations or capabilities.

In this section, we provide a brief overview of some of the emerging technology related issues in railroad operations. We specifically focus on PTC and EMS, but other emerging technologies (e.g., electronically controlled pneumatic brakes) could be used as examples as well. PTC and EMS are two of the most anticipated emerging technologies in the rail industry. PTC, mandated by RSIA (2008), is technology intended to ensure train separation, speed enforcement, and rail worker wayside safety. EMS provides train handling guidance to optimize fuel use. We draw on some of the results from the FRA-sponsored CTA summarized in Section 3 to point to the kinds of issues that will need to be explored as part of a comprehensive HSI process for acquiring and implementing new technologies. The types of questions and issues raised in this section are likely to come up with the introduction of any new technology in the railroad industry. They are intended to be representative of the types of questions that must be addressed for successful implementation of new technologies.

In the case of PTC and EMS, the functions and characteristics of the systems are already defined. Therefore, an important initial question is: what is the role of the train crew in interacting with these systems and with one another, and how will train crew roles and responsibilities be affected? These questions can best be addressed by first understanding the roles and responsibilities of locomotive engineers and conductors in today's environment and then exploring how the introduction of the new technologies are likely to impact those roles. For example, a question that motivated the conductor CTA was how PTC was likely to impact the role of conductors. The CTA found that PTC (as envisioned at the time of the CTA) would not account for all of the cognitive and physical support functions that conductors provide (Rosenhand, Roth and Multer, 2012). In the future, railroads need to continue asking this question as the role of the technology and train crew evolve. Will railroads transition to one-person operations? If so, they will need to address how the various physical and cognitive functions that are currently being performed by conductors will be handled—by automated systems or by other personnel). In addition, more exhaustive CTAs that consider the dynamic moment-by-moment workload and attention demands that arise while running a train may need to be performed to help system designers better understand the implications of transitioning to one-person operations.

To expand upon the previous question, will the engineer still be responsible for manually operating the train? If not, when will the engineer manually control the train? When will the software (automation) system operate the train with the engineer acting as supervisor? And, when will the roles be blended? Answers to these questions may introduce additional concerns. For example, situational awareness and operator vigilance may become more of a concern when the engineer's role becomes more supervisory.

Another objective related to the introduction of PTC, EMS, and other technologies is ensuring that the entire crew (not just the locomotive engineer) maintains situational awareness. From the roadway worker CTA, we know that roadway workers, dispatchers, and train crews have developed informal, cooperative strategies that foster shared situational awareness and create safety nets. How will the introduction of new technology impact these types of informal communication strategies that have become crucial for performance and safety?

To what extent will information that was previously obtained from outside the cab (along the wayside) be acquired from new displays? How should train crews divide their attention between displays inside the cab and information outside the cab? How will the need to monitor new technology affect engineer workload or distraction? The locomotive engineer CTA, which looked at PTC specifically, found that PTC (as it was designed at the time of the report) created new sources of workload and distraction, including the need to acknowledge frequent (and often non informative) audio alerts and the need for extensive input to the PTC system (Roth and Multer, 2007). PTC has since been redesigned; however, workload and distraction are still things to consider when introducing new technology.

When systems are developed separately to address different problems (as is the case with PTC and EMS), it is important to ensure that, when being used concurrently, they interact in acceptable ways. HSI methods may help to determine whether or not these systems are compatible with each other. For example, PTC and EMS both provide the engineer with speed guidance, but what happens when they provide conflicting information? How does the engineer decide which system to obey? As systems are being prototyped and tested in the field, conducting CTAs that employ field observations and interviews may provide information that helps answer these questions.

What is the design strategy when technology is incorporated in an evolutionary way? Currently, new technology and legacy systems frequently have to coexist. How long will this synchronicity work before it breaks down? What are the symptoms or problems that occur when this system begins to create more problems than it solves, or introduces new risks that cannot be addressed without throwing out the current design and starting over?

As new technology is introduced, does the nature of the work become more or less complex? Will there be a need for more or less training? The locomotive engineer CTA found that a substantial learning curve exists to reach the point where the in-cab display does not serve as a source of distraction. The findings suggest that engineers need sufficient training and experience running a PTC-equipped train to get beyond the point where close monitoring of the in-cab display is required to avoid a penalty brake application (Roth and Multer, 2007). However, more studies must be done to understand how PTC and EMS will be used by the train crew, and how the systems will interact with each other.

Performing safety and hazard analyses early on will allow us to better anticipate and address human performance issues that may have safety consequences. Wreathall, Roth, Bley, and Multer (2003) provide a model for how operating experience review, including cognitive task analyses, can be used to inform human reliability analyses as part of safety analyses conducted in support of product safety plan submissions. Wreathall, Roth, Bley, and Multer (2007) provide a roadmap of specific human factors concerns and their implications for safety analysis and risk assessment that should be considered in evaluating the introduction of new technologies, particularly processor-based signal and train control systems. The scope of factors that need to be considered range from implications for changes in operating practice, maintenance related safety concerns, to need for consideration of integration with existing systems, and interoperability issues across railroads.

The answers to the questions raised in this report, although unknown at this time, will influence the design considerations for displays and controls and effect changes to operating practices and training procedures. Conducting CTAs as part of a comprehensive HSI approach will ensure that the right questions are raised and that they are addressed through systematic analyses. This is essential, given that infrastructure and equipment in the railroad industry last a long time and decisions made today will affect train crews for years to come. Exploring the critical issues and anticipating potential risks will better enable railroads to produce optimal design and implementation plans, which will ultimately help us to better integrate these new technologies to ensure safety and efficiency in the short term and avoid costly fixes in the future.

5. CONCLUSIONS

CTA methods can play an important role as part of an HSI approach to supporting technology development and acquisition. The examples drawn from prior FRA CTAs illustrate how insights gained from CTAs can inform the development and deployment of new technologies. CTAs can help identify cognitive and collaborative activities that require more effective support, identify the kinds of aid that would be most effective (i.e., the type of information that is needed and how it can best be presented), and identify design pitfalls to avoid (i.e., potential negative side effects, or new cognitive and collaborative demands associated with the new technology that need to be addressed).

Conducting a CTA can help mitigate the risk of design failures by promoting a more complete understanding of how railroad employees work and the requirements necessary to support their safe and effective performance. This more complete understanding can help eliminate common design errors such as local optimizations, where too narrow a focus on improving a single aspect of a system in isolation can inadvertently lead to degradation of the overall system because of unanticipated side effects.

CTAs are particularly useful during the early phases of design when the goal is to understand the broader context of work so as to understand design needs and challenges. CTA methods continue to be relevant throughout the system development process, up to and including when systems are fielded to ensure that the intended benefits of the new technologies are realized and that unintended side effects (e.g., new forms of error, or new vulnerabilities to risk) are identified and mitigated. CTAs can be used to guide mid-course design corrections, as well as to lay the foundation for next-generation system development.

An important benefit of using CTA to inform system design is a reduction in risk exposure. This includes reducing the risk that the design will fail to meet the user's needs and therefore not be adopted, as well as reducing the risk that a design will be put in place that contributes to performance problems with costly economic and safety implications.

6. REFERENCES

Bisantz, A. M., Roth, E. M., Brickman, B., Gosbee, L., Hettinger, L., & McKinney, J. (2003). Integrating cognitive analyses in a large-scale system design process. *International Journal of Human-Computer Studies, 58,* 177–206.

Bisantz, A. & Roth, E. M. (2008). Analysis of Cognitive Work. In Deborah A. Boehm-Davis (Ed.) *Reviews of Human Factors and Ergonomics Volume 3.* Santa Monica, CA: Human Factors and Ergonomics Society. 1–43.

Booher, H. R. (2003). *Handbook of Human Systems Integration.* Hoboken, NJ: John Wiley & Sons, Inc.

Burns, C. M., Bisantz, A. M., & Roth, E. M. (2004). Lessons from a Comparison of Work Domain Models: Representational Choices and Their Implications. *Human Factors,* 46 (4), Winter 2004, pp 711–727.

Cook, R. I. & Woods, D. D. (1996a). Adapting to new technology in the operating room. *Human Factors,* 38, 593–613.

Cook, R. I. and Woods (1996b). Implications for automation surprises in aviation for the future of total intravenous anesthesia (TIVA). *Journal of Clinical Anesthesia,* 8, 29s–37s.

Cooke, N. J. (1994). Varieties of knowledge elicitation techniques. *International Journal of Human-Computer Studies, 41,* 801–849.

Crandall, B., Klein, G.A., & Hoffman, R.R. (2006). Working Minds: A Practitioner's Guide to Cognitive Task Analysis. Cambridge, MA: The MIT Press.

Dekker, S. W. A. (2002). *The field guide to human error investigation.* London: Ashgate.

Dekker, S. W. A. & Woods, D. D. (1999). To intervene or not to intervene: The dilemma of management by exception. *Cognition, Technology & Work, 1,* 86–96.

Elm, W.C., Potter, S.S., Gualtieri, J.W., Roth, E.M., & Easter, J.R. (2003). Applied Cognitive Work Analysis: A pragmatic Methodology for Designing Revolutionary Cognitive Affordances. In E. Hollnagel (Ed) *Handbook for Cognitive Task Design.* (pp. 357–382). London: Lawrence Erlbaum Associates, Inc.

Endsley, M., Bolté, B., & Jones, D. (2003). Designing for situation awareness: an approach to user-centered design. New York: Taylor & Francis.

Ericsson, K. A. & Simon, H. A. (1984). 1993. *Protocol analysis: Verbal reports as data.*

Flanagan, J. C. (1954). The critical incident technique. *Psychological Bulletin, 51,* 327–358.

Gray, W. D. & Kirschenbaum, S. S. (2000). Analyzing a novel expertise: An unmarked road. In

J. M. C. Schraagen, S. F. Chipman, & V. L. Shalin (Eds.), *Cognitive task analysis* (pp. 275–290.). Mahwah, NJ: Erlbaum.

Hoffman, R. (1987). The problem of extracting the knowledge of experts from the perspective of experimental psychology. *AI Magazine, 8* (Summer), 53–67.

Klein, G.A., Calderwood, R., & MacGregor, D. Critical Decision Method for Eliciting Knowledge. *IEEE Systems, Man, and Cybernetics SMC-19,* 462–472 (1989).

Klein, D. E., Klein, H. A., & Klein, G. (2000). Macrocognition: Linking Cognitive Psychology and Cognitive Ergonomics. *Proc. 5th Int'l Conf. Human Interactions with Complex Systems*, Univ. of Illinois at Urbana-Champaign, 2000, pp. 173–177.

Klein, G., Moon, B., & Hoffman, R. R. (2006). Making Sense of Sensemaking 1: Alternative Perspectives. *Intelligent Systems, IEEE, 21*(4), 70–73. doi: 10.1109/mis.2006.75.

Klein, G.A., Ross, K.G., Moon, B.M., Klein, D.E., Hoffman, R.R., & Hollnagel, E. (2003). Macrocognition. IEEE Intelligent Systems (May/June 2003), 81–84.

Klein, G. & Wolf, S. P. (1995). Decision-centered training. In *Proceedings of the Human Factors and Ergonomics Society 39th Annual Meeting* (pp. 1242–1252). Santa Monica, CA: Human Factors and Ergonomics Society.

Klinger, D. W. & Gomes, M. G. (1993). A cognitive systems engineering application for interface design. In *Proceedings of the Human Factors and Ergonomics Society 37th Annual Meeting.*

Malone, T., Savage-Knepshield, P., & Avery, L. (2007). Human-Systems Integration: Human Factors in a Systems Context. *Human Factors and Ergonomics Society Bulletin*, Vol. 50, #12, pp. 103.

Militello, L. & Hutton, R. (1998). Applied cognitive task analysis (ACTA): A practitioner's toolkit for understanding cognitive task demands. *Ergonomics, 41*(11), 1618–1641.

Mumaw, R. J., Roth, E. M., Vicente, K. J., & Burns, C. M. (2000). There is more to monitoring a nuclear power plant than meets the eye. *Human Factors, 42*(1), 36–55.

Naikar, N. (2006). Beyond interface design: Further applications of cognitive work analysis. *International Journal of Industrial Ergonomics, 36*(5), 423–438.

Naikar, N., Pearce, B., Drumm, D., & Sanderson, P. M. (2003). Designing Teams for First-of-a-Kind, Complex Systems Using the Initial Phases of Cognitive Work Analysis: Case Study. *Human Factors: The Journal of the Human Factors and Ergonomics Society, 45*(2), 202–217. doi: 10.1518/hfes.45.2.202.27236.

Naikar, N. & Sanderson, P. M. (2001). Evaluating Design Proposals for Complex Systems with Work Domain Analysis. *Human Factors: The Journal of the Human Factors and Ergonomics Society, 43*(4), 529-542. doi: 10.1518/001872001775870322.

National Research Council (NRC) Committee on Human-System Design Support for Changing Technology (2007). *Human-System Integration in the System Development Process.* National Academies Press. http://www.nap.edu/catalog.php?record_id=11893

Nehme, C.E., Scott, S.D., Cummings, M.L., & Furusho, C.Y. Generating Requirements for Futuristic Heterogeneous Unmanned Systems, Proceedings of HFES 2006: 50th Annual Meeting of the Human Factors and Ergonomic Society, San Francisco, CA, Oct., 2006.

Obradovich, J. & Woods, D. D. (1996). Users as designers: How people cope with poor HCI design in computer-based medical devices. *Human Factors*, 38, 574–592.

Obradovich, J. H. & Woods, D. D. (1996). SPECIAL SECTION: Users as Designers: How People Cope with Poor HCI Design in Computer-Based Medical Devices. *Human Factors: The Journal of the Human Factors and Ergonomics Society, 38*(4), 574–592.

O'Hara, J.M., Higgins, J.C., Persensky, J.J., Lewis, P.M., & Bongarra, J.P. (2004). *Human Factors Engineering Program Review Model.* Washington, DC: U.S. Nuclear Regulatory Commission/Office of Nuclear Regulatory Research.

O'Hara, J. M. & Roth, E. M. (2005). Operational concepts, teamwork, and technology in commercial nuclear power stations. In Clint Bowers, Eduardo Salas & Florian Jentsch (Eds) *Creating High-Tech Teams: Practical guidance on work performance and technology.* (pp. 139–159). Washington, DC: American Psychological Association.

Patterson, E. S., Cook, R. I., & Render, M. L. (2002). Improving Patient Safety by Identifying Side Effects from Introducing Bar Coding in Medication Administration. *Journal of the American Medical Informatics Association, 9*(5), 540–553. doi: 10.1197/jamia.M1061.

Patterson, E. S., Roth, E. M., & Woods, D. D. (2001). Predicting vulnerability in computer-supported inferential analysis under data overload. *Cognition, Technology & Work, 3,* 224–237.

Patterson, E. S., Roth, E. M., & Woods, D. D. (2010). Facets of complexity in situated work. In E. S. Patterson & J. Miller (Eds.) *Macrocognition Metrics and Scenarios: Design and Evaluation for Real-World Teams.* Ashgate Publishing. ISBN 978-0-7546-7578-5.

Potter, S. S., Roth, E. M., Woods, D., & Elm, W. C. (2000). Bootstrapping multiple converging cognitive task analysis techniques for system design. In J. M. Schraagen, S. F. Chipman, & V. L. Shalin (Eds.), *Cognitive Task Analysis.* Mahwah, NJ: Erlbaum.

Rasmussen, J. Information Processing, and Human-Machine Interaction: An Approach to Cognitive Engineering, Elsevier Science (North-Holland), New York, 1986.

Rasmussen, J., Pejtersen A., & Goodstein L., *Cognitive Systems Engineering*. New York: JohnWiley & Sons, Inc., 1994.

Reinach, S. & Jones, M. (2007). *An Introduction to Human Systems Integration (HSI) in the U.S. Railroad Industry*. Washington, DC: U.S. Department of Transportation, Federal Railroad Administration. http://www.fra.dot.gov/eLib/details/L03032

Rosenhand H., Roth E., & Multer, J. (2011). Cognitive and Collaborative Demands of Freight Conductor Activities: Results and Implications of a Cognitive Task Analysis. *Proceedings of the Human Factors and Ergonomics Society Annual Meeting*. Las Vegas, NV: Human Factors and Ergonomics Society. Proceedings of the Human Factors and Ergonomics Society Annual Meeting. September 2011. Vol 55 no 1. http://ntl.bts.gov/lib/43000/43000/43004/Rosenhand_cognition.pdf

Rosenhand H., Roth E., & Multer J. (2012). *Cognitive and Collaborative Demands of Freight Conductor Activities: Results and Implications of a Cognitive Task Analysis.* (DOT/FRA/ORD-12/13). Cambridge, MA, U.S. DOT Volpe National Transportation Systems Center. http://ntl.bts.gov/lib/46000/46100/46162/TR_Cognitive_Collaborative_Demands_Freight _Conductor_Activities_edited_FINAL_10_9_12.pdf

Roth, E. M. (2008). Uncovering the Requirements of Cognitive Work. *Human Factors*, 50 (3), 475–480. (Golden Anniversary Special Section on Discoveries and Developments).

Roth, E. M. & Bisantz, A. M. (2013). Cognitive Work Analysis. In Lee, J. D. & Kirlik, A. (Eds). The Oxford Handbook of Cognitive Engineering. Oxford University Press.

Roth, E. M., Lin, L., Kerch, S., Kenney, S. J., & Sugibayashi, N. (2001). Designing a first-of-a kind group view display for team decision making: a case study. In Salas, E. & Klein, G. (Eds) *Linking Expertise and Naturalistic Decision Making* (pp. 113–135). Mahwah, NJ: Lawrence Erlbaum Associates, Inc.

Roth, E. M., Malsch, N., & Multer, J. (2001). Understanding how train dispatchers manage and control trains: Results of a cognitive task analysis. Washington, DC: U.S. Department of Transportation, Federal Railroad Administration. (DOT/FRA/ORD-01/02). http://ntl.bts.gov/lib/33000/33600/33672/33672.pdf

Roth, E. M. & Mumaw, R. J. (1995). Using Cognitive Task Analysis to Define Human Interface Requirements for First-of-a-Kind Systems. Proceedings of the Human Factors and Ergonomics Society 39th Annual Meeting, San Diego, CA, Oct. 9–13, 1995. (pp. 520–524).

Roth, E. M., Multer, J., & Raslear, T. (2006). Shared situation awareness as a contributor to high reliability performance in railroad operations. *Organization Studies*, 27(7), 967–987. DOI: http://dx.doi.org/10.1177/1054773804271935

Roth, E., & Multer, J. (2007). Communication and Coordination Demands of Railroad Roadway Worker Activities and Implications for New Technology. Washington, DC: U.S. Department of Transportation, Federal Railroad Administration (DOT/FRA/ORD-07/28). Retrieved from http://www.fra.dot.gov/eLib/details/L01602

Roth, E. M., & Multer, J. (2009). Technology Implications of a Cognitive Task Analysis for Locomotive Engineers. Washington, DC: U.S. Department of Transportation, Federal Railroad Administration (DOT/FRA/ORD-09/03) http://www.volpe.dot.gov/coi/hfrsa/docs/tiocrafle.pdf

Roth, E. M. & Patterson, E. S. (2005). Using observational study as a tool for discovery: Uncovering cognitive and collaborative demands and adaptive strategies. In Montgomery, H., Lipshitz, R., & Brehmer, B. (Eds.) *How professionals make decisions*. (pp. 379–393) Mahwah, NJ: Lawrence Erlbaum Associates.

Roth, E., M., Scott, R., Deutsch, S., Kuper, S., Schmidt, V., Stilson, M., & Wampler, J. (2006). Evolvable work-centered support systems for command and control: Creating systems users can adapt to meet changing demands. *Ergonomics*, vol. 49, #7, 688–705.

Roth, E. M., Stilson, M., Scott, R., Whitaker, R., Kazmierczak, T., Thomas-Meyers, G. & Wampler, J. (2006). Work-centered design and evaluation of a C2 Visualization Aid. *Proceedings of the Human Factors and Ergonomics Society 50th Annual Meeting*. (pp. 255–259). Santa Monica, CA: Human Factors and Ergonomics Society.

Roth, E. M., & Woods, D. D. (1988). Aiding human performance 1: Cognitive analysis. *Le Travail Humain, 41*(1), 39–64.

Schraagen, J. M., Chipman, S. F., & Shalin, V. L. (Eds.). (2000). *Cognitive Task Analysis*. Mahwah, NJ: Lawrence Erlbaum Associates.

Schaafstal, A., Schraagen, J. M., & van Berlo, M. (2000). Cognitive task analysis and innovation of training: The case of structured troubleshooting. *Human Factors, 42*, 75–86.

Smith, P., Woods, D. D., McCoy, E., Billings, C. E., Sarter, N. B., Dennings, R., et al (1998). Using forecasts of future incidents to evaluate future ATM system designs. Air Traffic Control Quarterly, 6(1), 71–85.

Tappan, J.M., Pitman, D.J., Abi Akar, C., & Cummings, M.L. (2011). Minimum Information Interface for Locomotive Operations (MIILO) Final Report, (HAL2010-04), MIT Humans and Automation Laboratory, Cambridge, MA.

Vicente, K.J., *Cognitive Work Analysis: Toward Safe, Productive, and Healthy Computer-based Work*, Lawrence Erlbaum Associates, Mahwah, NJ, 1999.

Watson, M. O. & Sanderson, P. M. (2007). Designing for attention with sound: Challenges and extensions to ecological interface design. *Human Factors, 49*, 331–346.

Woods, D. D. (1993). Process tracing methods for the study of cognition outside of the experimental psychology laboratory. In G. A. Klein, J. Orasanu, R. Calderwood & C. E. Zsambok (Eds.), *Decision-making in action: Models and methods* (pp. 228–251). Norwood, NJ: Ablex.

Woods, D. & Dekker, S. (2000). Anticipating the effects of technological change: A new era of dynamics for human factors. *Theoretical Issues in Ergonomics Science, 1*(3), 272–282.

Woods, D. D. & Hollnagel, E. (2006). *Joint cognitive systems: Patterns in cognitive systems engineering.* Boca Raton, FL: Taylor & Francis.

Woods, D. D. & Roth, E. M. (1988). Cognitive engineering: Human problem solving with tools. *Human Factors*, 30 (4), pp. 415–430.

Wreathall, J., Roth, E., Bley, D., & Multer, J. (2003). *Human Reliability Analysis in Support of Risk Assessment for Positive Train Control.* Report No. DOT/FRA/ORD-03/15. U.S. Department of Transportation, Federal Railroad Administration, Washington, DC. http://www.fra.dot.gov/eLib/details/L03551

Wreathall, J., Woods, D. D., Bing, A. J. & Christoffersen, K. (2007). Relative risk of workload transitions in positive train control. Washington, DC: U.S. Department of Transportation, Federal Railroad Administration. DOT/FRA/ORD-07/12. http://ntl.bts.gov/lib/42000/42400/42472/ord0712.pdf

Wreathall, J., Roth, E., Bley, D. & Multer, J. (2007). Human factors considerations in the evaluation of processor-based signal and train control systems. Washington, DC: U.S. Department of Transportation, Federal Railroad Administration. DOT/FRA/ORD-07/07. http://www.fra.dot.gov/eLib/details/L01620